Cambridge Elements

Elements in Politics and Communication
edited by
Stuart Soroka
University of Michigan

THE INCREASING
VIABILITY OF GOOD NEWS

Stuart Soroka
University of Michigan

Yanna Krupnikov
Stony Brook University

CAMBRIDGE
UNIVERSITY PRESS

University Printing House, Cambridge CB2 8BS, United Kingdom

One Liberty Plaza, 20th Floor, New York, NY 10006, USA

477 Williamstown Road, Port Melbourne, VIC 3207, Australia

314–321, 3rd Floor, Plot 3, Splendor Forum, Jasola District Centre, New Delhi – 110025, India

103 Penang Road, #05–06/07, Visioncrest Commercial, Singapore 238467

Cambridge University Press is part of the University of Cambridge.

It furthers the University's mission by disseminating knowledge in the pursuit of education, learning, and research at the highest international levels of excellence.

www.cambridge.org
Information on this title: www.cambridge.org/9781108987080
DOI: 10.1017/9781108982375

First published 2021

A catalogue record for this publication is available from the British Library.

ISBN 978-1-108-98708-0 Paperback
ISSN 2633-9897 (online)
ISSN 2633-9889 (print)

The Increasing Viability of Good News

Elements in Politics and Communication

DOI:10.1017/9781108982375
First published online: June 2021

Stuart Soroka
University of Michigan

Yanna Krupnikov
Stony Brook University

Author for correspondence: Stuart Soroka, snsoroka@ucla.edu

Abstract: In spite of what appears to be the increasingly negative tone of media coverage, this Element suggests that the prevalence of positive news is likely to increase, for three reasons: (1) valence-based asymmetries vary over time, (2) valence-based asymmetries vary across individuals, and (3) technology facilitates diverse news platforms catering to diverse preferences. Each of these claims is examined in detail here, based on analyses of prior and/or novel data on media content, psychophysiological responses, and survey-based experiments. Results are considered as they relate to our understanding of media gatekeeping, political communication, and political psychology, and also as actionable findings for producers of media content, communications platforms, and media consumers.

Keywords: political communication, news, journalism, positivity, negativity bias

ISBNs:9781108987080 (PB), 9781108982375 (OC)
ISSNs:2633-9897 (online), 2633-9889 (print)

Contents

1 Introduction

Our information environment is changing. Shifts in technology are facilitating fundamental transformations in the kinds of information to which we regularly have access. There are more readily available pet pictures, baby pictures, and celebratory bread-making pictures now than at any time in recent history. There is simultaneously more sensationalistic, negative, polarizing, and intentionally misleading news content. The former is at least in part a product of the latter – the Internet has created an infinite amount of space waiting to be filled with content, after all. This is a central theme of the pages that follow.[1]

This Element is partly a response to the environment in which it was started, several months into the 2020 COVID-19 pandemic, in the midst of protests following the police killing of George Floyd, and in the lead-up to the 2020 US presidential election. But the idea developed here was in evidence long before the appearance of the novel coronavirus and heightened news attentiveness to the Black Lives Matter (BLM) movement. There has for some time been concern that mass media are so inclined toward negative and/or sensationalistic and/or conflict-laden content that we will soon be entirely consumed by it. Given the past few years (or even the past few months) of news coverage, this prediction is well worth considering. There is, after all, a considerable body of work suggesting that media competition drives up negativity and sensationalism (e.g., Dunaway 2008, 2013), and an online news environment in which competition for audiences is considerable. There also is a burgeoning literature on the increasing attention given to "fake" news – news that typically capitalizes on human biases toward negative, sensationalistic, and conflict-laden information. Political polarization appears to be on the rise (e.g., Iyengar et al. 2019), and misinformation is prevalent (although thus far limited in impact; see, e.g., Guess et al. 2019). Even in the midst of a viral pandemic, wearing a face mask has turned into a contested political statement (Druckman et al. 2021).

---

[1] Much of our thinking on this topic has been affected by collaborative projects over the past decade. Research on outlyingness as a driver of attention to information was developed with P. J. Lamberson. Work on differences in information across media platforms was done in collaboration with Mark Daku, Lauren Guggenheim, Dan Hiaeshutter-Rice, Patrick Kraft, Kerri Milita, Josh Pasek, and John Barry Ryan. Psychophysiological studies of negativity biases were conducted with Patrick Fournier, Lilach Nir, Johanna Dunaway, Kevin Arceneaux, and Bert Bakker. All of this work features prominently in what follows. Our argument here has also benefited from conversations and advice from Sarah Bachleda Fioroni, Dan Hiaeshutter-Rice, Ariel Hasell, Patrick Fournier, Michael Wagner and Brian Weeks and from presentations in the Department of Communication and Media at the University of Michigan, the Department of Communication at the University of California, Los Angeles, the Department of Government at the University of Texas at Austin, and the Hot Politics Lab at the Amsterdam School of Communication Research, University of Amsterdam.

Is it our destiny to be surrounded by overwhelmingly negative news content? Our answer in the pages that follow is *No*. Human interests vary over time and across individuals. Technology increasingly facilitates information consumption that reflects these interests, sometimes with perverse consequences, but often with advantages as well. One such advantage is the increasing number of at-home singing and dancing videos and we're-in-this-together tweets.

We make our case in the following stages. We begin with a consideration of the valence of newspaper coverage in roughly sixty-two thousand news stories over the first eight months of 2020, with a focus on content related to both COVID-19 and BLM. We then consider the valence of more than three hundred thousand television news stories over the past thirty years. Trends in both newspaper and television coverage highlight the tendency for the valence of news to be "self-correcting" – to display very negative valence at some points, to be sure, but also to return to a more mildly negative equilibrium shortly thereafter. Why does this matter? Why does it happen? We consider the first of these questions by revisiting past work on the normative and empirical implications that the "valence" of information has for engagement, participation, preferences, and information processing. We argue that we should be interested in "valence-based asymmetries" in news coverage (i.e., the tendency for content to be predominantly positive or negative) because we know that valence matters for behavior and well-being, political and otherwise. The bulk of our monograph then focuses on the second question, and moreover on the possibility that the volume and availability of positively valenced news is likely to increase rather than decrease.

That possibility is, we believe, driven by three factors:

(1) *Valence-based asymmetries vary over time.* There is variation in valence-based asymmetries across time, driven by outlyingness, novelty, and/or adaptive processing.

(2) *Valence-based asymmetries vary across individuals.* Different people process information differently. We all have long-standing systematic biases in information selection, and in the ways in which we respond to that information.

(3) *Technology facilitates diverse news platforms catering to diverse preferences.* Technology is facilitating the ready availability of information that varies in many different ways – by topic, by political ideology, and by valence as well. The proliferation of platforms increasingly allows media consumers to move between sources in order to achieve an "ideal" balance of positive and news content. Media may well adapt by producing more

positive content; this may be seen at the level of individual media outlets, but it may be especially evident looking at "media" as a whole.

This three-part argument is somewhat more optimistic about the future of media content than is typical, at least at the present time. It also is partly a response to our own prior work, which has focused on the prevalence of negative campaigns and news content (e.g., Krupnikov 2011; Krupnikov and Piston 2015), and the related tendency for humans to be more attentive to and affected by negative rather than positive information (e.g., Soroka 2014). That work is most often focused on the central tendency – the average – across humans and over time. The argument that follows concentrates more on the variation around that average. Acknowledging this variation is an important step toward understanding why our information environment is in fact not inevitably overwhelmingly negative, and why there are at the present time reasons to expect an increasing rather than decreasing volume of good news.

Note that our argument should not be confused with one about future news events. We do not expect miraculous cures for deadly diseases or an end to injustice. Rather, we believe that even in a context marked by negativity and sadness, news content that focuses on positive events – even if these events are minor – will increasingly emerge. Put differently, our argument is not that good news will emerge because the course of human history will turn in a positive direction (this may turn out to be so, but we simply do not know), but rather that the news environment will increasingly search out and make room for more positively valenced content.

2 The Valence of News Coverage

The "valence" of news coverage refers to the degree to which the information is affectively positive or negative. In some instances, valence is easily established. News about sickness and death is almost always perceived as negative by everyone, for instance. Increasing unemployment is almost always perceived as negative news, while news about decreasing unemployment is almost always perceived as good news (Soroka 2006). But there are always individuals with different viewpoints. A wealthy, well-employed minority may see rising unemployment as advantageous insofar as it is linked to decreasing inflation, for instance. Partisan groups will often see policy outcomes through very different lenses. The valence of information is rarely purely objective. It can be more or less subjective, but it is almost always at least partly a matter of perspective.

Distinguishing between primarily *objective* versus primarily *subjective* valence is possible, and often critical in research that seeks to examine responses to negative and positive information. Acknowledging that a large amount of mediated information may be positive or negative to different people is important. The distribution of valence in mediated information is different for everyone, at least in part because our perceptions of the valence of information vary. There nevertheless are limits to this subjectivity. It is very unlikely that people look at news coverage in the midst of a pandemic, with rising unemployment and the current second/third wave of a virus, and think that news content is mostly positively valenced.[2] Indeed, our shared assessment of the valence of mediated information is revealed in the considerable body of work that links media coverage to public attitudes. Regardless of the direction of the causal effect (see, e.g., Wlezien and Soroka 2018), either positive and negative media coverage has an impact on public attitudes, or positive and negative public attitudes are regularly reflected in the language of news. In order for either of these to be the case – and plenty of evidence suggests that they are (e.g., Dalton et al. 1998; Hopmann et al. 2010; Shaw 1999; Soroka et al. 2009, 2015) – there *has* to be some shared sense of what information is negative and what information is positive.

There are in addition good reasons to consider the valence of news above and beyond its substantive content. Living in complex, information-rich environments requires that we develop simple, fast mechanisms for categorizing and paying attention to (or not) information. The human brain is thus finely tuned to quickly recognize and respond to the valence of information (e.g., Zajonc 1980), and in some instances affective responses may matter more to our decision-making than "cognitive" assessments of incoming information (e.g., Loewenstein et al. 2001). The quick recognition of valence is central to what Kahneman (2013) famously describes as System 1 (fast, automatic, affective, unconscious) thinking versus System 2 (slow, deliberative, conscious) thinking. And his argument builds on a considerable body of prior work, including Epstein's (1994) discussion of "experiential" versus "analytical" thinking, Damasio's research on "somatic markers" (2005), and Slovic et al.'s (2002) work on the "affect heuristic." A growing body of neurological work further highlights the relative significance of and speed with which the human brain responds to the valence of information (e.g., Bayer et al. 2010; Feng et al. 2014; Gianotti et al. 2008).

This is not to say that we do not have substantive interests – some people are interested in news about football and others are not. But our decision to look for, select, and/or respond to information will often be conditioned in the first

---

[2] Petersen et al. (2020) suggest that some citizens purposefully circulate fake news out of a "need for chaos." They may consequently derive some enjoyment from circulating negative information. But even these readers likely recognize that the information is negatively valenced.

instance by the valence of that information. Indeed, in many cases we may prioritize the valence of news over the actual substance; or, to push this line of thinking even further, sometimes the valence is the substance. To paraphrase Marshall McLuhan: *the mood is the message*. For this reason, a consideration of (just) the valence of news is of some importance.

What, then, is the valence of current-affairs news coverage? Note that current-affairs news coverage is a small proportion of media content, particularly when "media content" includes information circulating on social media. In the closing section we consider what our argument might look like in a multi-platform media environment that is predominantly not about current affairs. For the time being, however, we focus on news, primarily in "traditional" or "legacy" newspaper and broadcast outlets. And on this front there are vast literatures detailing the tendency for this content to be sensationalistic (typically in a negative way; see, e.g., Davie and Lee 1995; Harmon 1989; Hofstetter and Dozier 1986; Ryu 1982), problem-oriented (Altheide 1997), and negative more broadly (e.g., Benoit et al. 2005; Diamond 1978; Fallows 1997; Farnsworth and Lichter 2007; Just et al. 1996; Kerbel 1995; Lichter and Noyes 1996; Niven 2000; Patterson 1994; Sabato 1991).

Has this negativity been increasing over time? Let us consider two different exhibits based on news coverage over the past forty years. The first is relatively recent. Figure 1 shows the frequency and sentiment of newspaper coverage of COVID-19 and the BLM movement over the first eight months of 2020. We focus on this coverage for several reasons. First, COVID-19 and BLM form the two uniquely defining news stories of 2020. Second, these two stories are founded on negative events. Coverage of COVID-19 begins with a global pandemic that costs millions of people their lives; coverage of BLM begins with police brutality and racial injustice. These stories, then, form notable examples – journalists would need to work deliberately to include positivity in this coverage.

The data in Figure 1 are drawn from the Lexis-Nexis full-text news archive and include all stories in the front sections of the *New York Times*, *Washington Post*, and *LA Times*, alongside all coverage in the *Atlanta Journal-Constitution*, *Minneapolis Star Tribune*, *Philadelphia Inquirer*, and *USA Today*. (We focus on front sections for the first three papers due to the size of those papers; the latter three have, in contrast, much less content to download and analyze.) From that database, we identify every news story about either COVID-19 or the BLM movement using a simple keyword search.[3] Any article that does not fall into one of these categories is placed in the "other" category.

---

[3] The keyword search is very straightforward. Any article with more than one mention of "COVID," "coronavirus," or "pandemic" is identified as a COVID-19 article. Any article with more than one mention of "Black Lives Matter" or "BLM" is identified as a BLM article. Note

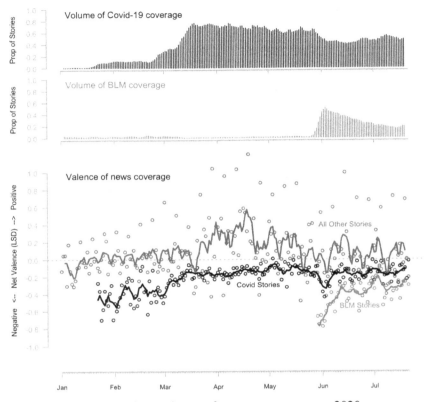

Figure 1 The sentiment of newspaper coverage, 2020

Based on COVID and BLM stories in the *Atlanta Journal-Constitution*, *Los Angeles Times*, *New York Times*, *Minneapolis Star-Tribune*, *Philadelphia Inquirer*, *USA Today*, and *Washington Post*. The line shows a rolling center-weighted five-day average. Sentiment is based on the LSD, as implemented in quanteda in R. Net sentiment is calculated as follows: log [(pos. counts + 0.5) / (neg. counts + 0.5)].

Data are analyzed at the story level, and the valence of stories is estimated using the Lexicoder Sentiment Dictionary (LSD) (Young and Soroka, 2012). The LSD is composed of roughly five thousand words, half positive and half negative. We estimate counts of positive and negative words using the implementation of the LSD in the quanteda package in R (Benoit et al. 2018). We then produce an estimate of "net sentiment" using a measure suggested in Lowe et al. (2011) and used in Proksch et al. (2019), as follows: log [(pos. counts + 0.5) /

---

that we require *more than one* mention of either of these words in order to categorize an article as COVID-19 or BLM. This is because a large number of articles during this period mentioned one or the other topic very briefly in passing. (This was especially true for COVID-19.) Our intention here was thus to separate out the articles that actually discuss one or the other topic.

(neg. counts + 0.5)]. This is an empirical logit, slightly smoothed toward zero, and very highly correlated with another standard approach: (pos. counts − neg. counts) / total words. The resulting net sentiment is greater than zero when positive words outnumber negative words, and less than zero when negative words outnumber positive ones.[4]

The top panels of Figure 1 do not focus on the valence but rather on the volume of news coverage of both COVID-19 and BLM. In mid-March, nearly 80 percent of our sample of news coverage mentions COVID-19 multiple times, and even at the end of July nearly 50 percent of news coverage is focused on COVID-19. This is to be expected. Although cases of the coronavirus had been documented in the United States as early as January, cases spiked in March, leading states to implement numerous mitigation policies. Attention to BLM peaks in early June, when roughly 50 percent of coverage includes multiple mentions of BLM. This timing is also reflective of news events: George Floyd was killed on May 25, 2020, which led to protests in late May. (Note that the COVID-19 and BLM categories are not mutually exclusive – articles can be and regularly are about both.)

What is the valence of these articles, and how does it compare with the valence of articles *not* about either COVID-19 or BLM? The bottom panel of Figure 1 shows the average valence of our three different categories of news articles daily. Circles show daily averages; lines show a rolling center-weighted five-day average for each category. There are in our view three trends especially worth highlighting.

First, although the valence of COVID-19 coverage is markedly negative to start, it becomes more positive through March and then remains at that moderately negative level for the subsequent four months. In fact, comparing the top and bottom panels of Figure 1, the valence of COVID-19 coverage improves at roughly the same time as it becomes highly salient. The less negative valence of COVID-19 coverage is also accompanied by roughly sixty days (from mid-March to mid-May) of decidedly positive *not* COVID-19 coverage. The end result is that the complexion of news coverage at the height of the pandemic is

---

[4] Past work suggests that the LSD is as reliable if not more reliable for news content than other general-purpose sentiment dictionaries (Young and Soroka 2012). Recent work highlights some advantages of sentiment tools that rely on a combination of human coding and machine learning (Van Atteveldt et al. n.d.). Note that corpus-specific machine learning-based tools should in most cases be more accurate than a general-purpose dictionary. The dictionary has typically been tested on another corpus, after all, while the machine learning typically relies on the specific corpus under investigation. To be clear: the central difference may be less about dictionaries versus machines, and more about general-purpose versus corpus-specific approaches. Regardless, at the very high level of aggregation used here the differences between various dictionaries and machine-learning approaches tend to be minimized.

not as negative as we might anticipate, and on balance it is slightly more positive than before the pandemic.

A similar dynamic is evident for coverage of BLM. Coverage of BLM is initially very negative, but that negativity is cut in half after the first two weeks of protests. There is no point at which BLM coverage is positive on average, and it is more negative than COVID-19 coverage throughout June and July. But like coverage of COVID-19, the initial negativity of BLM coverage dissipates relatively quickly.

What accounts for the seemingly fast moderation of the negativity in news coverage of two ongoing, long-standing, and mostly not improving phenomena? There are surely multiple drivers. Widespread misunderstandings about the magnitude and severity of the COVID-19 pandemic were likely one source of decreased negativity in COVID-19 coverage, for instance, just as systematic racism likely muted prolonged attentiveness to the problems highlighted by the BLM movement. But we also suspect that the positive shift in the valence of 2020 news coverage is a common phenomenon – evident in media reactions to a wide range (if not all) of the major problems over the past few decades.

Consider, for instance, Figure 2, which shows the trend in the valence of television news coverage over the past thirty years. The analysis in this instance is based on the full transcript of every evening newscast from 1990 onward on ABC, CBS, and NBC, extracted from the Lexis-Nexis database. As in Figure 1, circles in Figure 2 show the average sentiment across all stories on all three

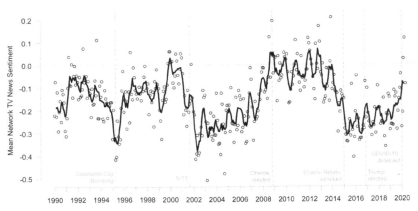

Figure 2 The sentiment of network news, 1990–2018

Circles show the monthly averages for all stories on national nightly news programs on ABC, CBS, and NBC. The line shows a rolling center-weighted five-month average. Sentiment is based on the LSD, as implemented in quanteda in R. Net sentiment is calculated as follows: $\log [(\text{pos. counts} + 0.5) / (\text{neg. counts} + 0.5)]$.

networks monthly. The line shows a rolling five-month center-weighted average of these monthly values.

Note that the LSD does not distinguish between different types of negativity (see, e.g., Lengauer et al. 2012). Sentiment expressed by interviewees, commentary and evaluations by journalists, and the valence of the events themselves (i.e., deaths versus heroics) are all lumped together in this very general measure of the valence of the language of newscasts. The measure also does not distinguish between topics or themes – the economy, health care, the environment, and celebrity breakups are all pooled in the measure of sentiment shown here. This is purposeful. There most certainly are important differences between the information conveyed in reporting versus commentary, or political versus entertainment news. But all of this information has a valence – positive, negative, or neutral – and there are good reasons to believe that both news production and news consumption are powerfully affected by this critical aspect of content.

With this in mind, then, there are three features of Figure 2 worth noting. The first is prosaic but methodologically important: the peaks and troughs in Figure 2 correspond with events that we should expect to have a marked impact on media sentiment. Some of the most important moments are shown in Figure 2 using vertical lines. The Oklahoma City bombing, 9/11, and much of 2015 (beginning with the *Charlie Hebdo* shooting, followed by school shootings) stand out as particularly negative moments in TV network news. The month Obama was elected is the second most positive month in thirty years of TV reporting (surpassed only by the month in which Nelson Mandela's passing produces a large number of positive remembrances). George W. Bush begins his term in office with relatively positive media coverage, although this collapses quickly and never recovers. Obama's terms in office see comparatively positive media coverage, although coverage sours in 2015 due to events abroad and at home. All of these trends offer simple but important confirmations of the concurrent validity of the sentiment measure.

The second feature of Figure 2 worth noting is that the vast majority of months have an average sentiment that is well below zero. (Zero is shown in Figure 2 by a horizontal dotted line.) Of the 366 months for which we have data, just 42 (11 percent) have an average sentiment above zero. The tendency for negative words to outnumber positive words in media coverage is readily apparent in these data.

Is this a bad thing or a good thing? We really do not know. There are certainly reasons for concern about biases in the valence of news coverage. Consider first the normative concerns about systematically negative news coverage and political engagement. There are long-standing worries that negative news coverage contributes· to declining trust in political institutions and disengagement in politics (Farnsworth and Lichter 2007; Moy and Pfau 2000; Patterson 1994). Similar themes echo in work on "media malaise" in which the sentiment of news coverage decreases trust and political efficacy (e.g., Robinson 1976), and in work on the "spiral of cynicism" in which conflict-oriented coverage contributes to public cynicism about politics (e.g., Cappella and Hall-Jamieson 1997; Valentino et al. 2001).

That said, there also are reasons to expect negative news to increase attention to and engagement with politics. Indeed, work evaluating both the media malaise and the spiral of cynicism hypotheses has regularly finds evidence of the opposite possibility (e.g., Newton 1999; Strömbäck and Shehata 2010; de Vreese 2005). This makes sense given that people seem more interested in negative news content (e.g., Trussler and Soroka 2014). It may also be that the impact of affectively negative content has heterogeneous effects, depending in part on the specific negative emotion that content produces (e.g., Brader 2006; Nabi 1999; Valentino et al. 2009). There is of course a vast literature chronicling the heterogeneous and context- and candidate-dependent effects of negative political advertising (e.g., Fridkin and Kenney 2011; Krupnikov 2011, 2014; Krupnikov and Piston 2015). It is similarly unclear whether negative news content will on average increase or decrease our engagement with politics. We suspect that there is likely an "ideal point" where negativity in media coverage is concerned: there should be enough negativity to keep us interested, but not so much over time that we withdraw from news consumption and politics (Soroka 2014). Of course, we do not know what that "ideal point" is.

It also is unclear whether a bias toward negatively valenced content reflects journalism run amok or journalists doing their job. One account of negativity in news content emphasizes a post-Watergate increase in journalistic skepticism that produces systematically biased and cynical reporting (e.g., Patterson 1994). Another is that we expect media to act as a "Fourth Estate," monitoring and highlighting errors in representative government. Doing this necessarily produces media content focused on negative outcomes. Indeed, negative content may reflect greater levels of information than positive content insofar as that negativity reflects a critique or contrasting of political positions (e.g., Geer 2008). Moreover, there are times when media content quite clearly should be negative because current events are negative. It would be hard to sustain the argument that during a global pandemic media content is too negative. Sometimes, perhaps often, negatively valenced news accurately reflects the state of the world.

In short, it needn't be the case that negatively valenced media content will drive all citizens to withdraw from politics, nor is it necessarily a signal that media are providing a systematically biased view of public affairs. This is not to say that the valence of news coverage does not matter, just that the consequence of systematic tendencies in the valence of news coverage is complex. And past work makes clear that the valence of news coverage is central to our understanding of (a) whether we are attentive to that information, (b) how we process that information, and (c) how we behave in response to that information. For all of these reasons, understanding the dynamics of the valence of news coverage is of real significance.

It also is the case that, assuming there is an "ideal point" at which negativity grabs attention but is not yet demobilizing, we may have moved well beyond it. And the consequences may not be related just to attention to politics. There are long-standing – and now, it seems, especially prescient – concerns that systematically negative content decreases our psychological well-being (e.g., Bodas et al. 2015; Johnston and Davey 1997; Kinnick et al. 2016; Marin et al. 2012; Szabo and Hopkinson 2007; VanderWeele and Brooks 2020; Wormwood et al. 2019). There clearly are good reasons to consider the possibility that media are prioritizing negative content too much, to the detriment of our social, political, and psychological health.

This third feature of Figure 2 is thus of real significance: there has in fact *not* been a steady decline in the sentiment of US television coverage over the past thirty years.[5] There is meaningful variation, to be sure, and the past several years have seen news coverage that is roughly as negative as the first coverage of the War on Terror. But there have been similar low points through this time period, and high points throughout the past thirty years as well. (The COVID-19 pandemic appears to be a period of relatively positive news content, which may be surprising. Section 3.1 suggests several possible reasons for this finding.) But for the time being, the fact that there is no steady downward trend in the valence of news coverage over the past thirty years is important.

This is not to say that media content is not negative. It clearly is, most of the time. The *cumulative* impact of news coverage is also strikingly negative – and there is no sign in these data that cumulation of negative content will be significantly moderated by any extended period of positive content. Even so: (a) there is no strong trend toward increased negativity; (b) there is a steady trickle of positive news content; and (c) intermittently there are months in which positive content outweighs negative content.

Why does this positive content exist? One straightforward answer is that sometimes good things are happening in the world. Reality will itself lead to

---

[5] Nor is there an increase in the total number of sentiment-bearing words in the TV corpus. Over this thirty-year time period, the proportion of sentiment-bearing words varies between roughly 5 and 8 percent, with no systematic increase over time.

variation in the valence of news coverage over time. This is an incomplete account, however – there will at most times be positively and negatively valenced information, and past work finds that news coverage systematically favors the latter (e.g., Soroka 2006, 2012, 2014). One related possibility is that news organizations respond to two pressures from audiences: first, to provide attention-grabbing negative content, and second, to offer an accurate view of the world. The latter will in some instances overwhelm the former, and one consequence may be the appearance of positively valenced content. Even if news audiences typically prioritize negative information, sometimes good news powers through.

Another more broadly applicable account is that news coverage at any given time reflects a range of journalistic and audience interests. Journalists' and audiences' preferences vary over time and across individuals. It follows that there will be moments when, almost regardless of the valence of the "real world," news content will be partly or even predominantly positive. Why, then, might there be more positive content in the not too distant future? We develop our three-part answer in Section 3.

3 The Argument

If negative content draws an audience, and mass media (traditional and social) are seeking audiences, then why does good news exist at all? And why are there times at which good news dominates? There are three reasons.

3.1 Valence-Based Asymmetries Vary Over Time

Our argument that valence-based asymmetries vary over time is based on past work on (a) outlyingness, (b) novelty, and (c) adaptive processing. We consider each of these in turn.

3.1.1 Outlyingness

The crux of the argument about outlyingness, drawn largely from Lamberson and Soroka (2019), is as follows: it may be that it is not negativity per se that draws attention, but outlyingness. We are drawn to information that is at odds with our expectations. And, based on the literature discussed below, negative information tends to be at odds with our expectations because, on average, humans expect mildly positive information.

The arithmetic of this argument is simple. Imagine that the valence of information is captured by a scale running from −5 to +5. If we expect a 0 (neutral), then information that is +4 (positive) is no more or less outlying than information that is −4 (negative). But if we expect a +1, then +4 is only three steps upward and −4 is now five steps downward. Put differently, given that we expect +1, −4 is more outlying than +4. It follows that if we tend to have expectations that are > 0, negative information will tend to be more outlying.

The argument that outlyingness may matter for attentiveness has a long history, beginning with work in psychology on impression formation (e.g., Fiske 1980; Helson 1964; Sherif and Sherif 1967; Skowronski and Carlston 1989), and is also evident in work in neuroscience suggesting that the human brain has evolved to focus on unexpected information (e.g., Dragoi et al. 2002; Itti and Baldi 2009). Of course, attentiveness to outlying information is not enough to account for long-standing negativity biases – we also need long-standing positive expectations, that is, a positive baseline from which negative information is more outlying. That positive baseline is considered in the aforementioned literatures, but is examined most directly in psychological work on the "positivity offset" (e.g., Ito and Cacioppo 2005; Norris et al. 2011) – that is, the tendency for humans to evaluate neutral information as mildly positive, and/or respond more strongly to positive information than negative information at very low levels of input. Because of the positivity offset, we often evaluate information based on positive expectations. This makes negative information more outlying.

That said, our expectations change in response to incoming information. It can thus be true that even as most humans exhibit mildly positive expectations most of the time (and a negativity bias in response to new information as a result), there can be instances in which shifts in the baseline make negative information *less* outlying. Past work on adaptive expectations, primarily in economics, explores the impact of shifting baselines (e.g., Gooding et al. 1996; Hey 1994; Sterman 1987). Figure 3 illustrates the basic idea. Panel A shows the gap between expectations and a piece of positive information versus a piece of negative information, when expectations exhibit a positivity offset. In this instance, negative information is more outlying. If those expectations shift to the middle, however, as in Panel B, neither positive information nor negative information is more outlying. In Panel C, when expectations shift even further to the left, positive information is now more outlying than negative information.

Are there instances in which our expectations are better illustrated by C than by A? Lamberson and Soroka (2019) (see also Soroka 2014) find that news coverage of the economy exhibits this dynamic. There *are* times in the past twenty years when, due to durably poor economic circumstances, public expectations of the economy shifted downward; media and public responsiveness was greater to positive information than to negative information as a result. Put differently, when the economy is doing well, media (and humans) are more attentive to negative information. When the economy is doing poorly, media (and humans) are more attentive to positive information.

A. Negative Information is Outlying

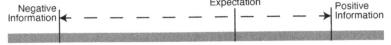

B. Balanced Information

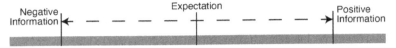

C. Positive Information is Outlying

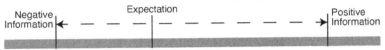

Figure 3 The impact of shifting expectations on the outlyingness of information

3.1.2 Novelty

Note that it is difficult to distinguish the importance of a shifting baseline from the importance of novelty. We may sometimes seek out outlying information because it deviates from our expectations and thus seems especially informative/diagnostic; alternatively, we may seek out information simply because it is different from what we have been consuming. There is a literature that focuses on novelty (e.g., Berger and Milkman 2012; Kim 2015), which expects roughly the same dynamic as illustrated in Figure 3. We nevertheless want to distinguish here between *outlyingness*, characterized by deviation from a long-term baseline expectation, and *novelty*, characterized by difference from information very recently consumed. Note that both might produce the dynamic shown in Figure 3. And both may be happening at the same time: our baseline expectations shift slowly, but we also sometimes just get bored of a certain type of information.

Either outlyingness from a baseline or a desire for novelty could produce interest in more positive news content. By our definition, the long-term change examined in Lamberson and Soroka (2019) is driven by the former. It may be possible to observe the latter as well.

Consider the structure of a typical evening newscast. As Figure 2 makes clear, this content is on average negative. But the typical American newscast shifts in valence from beginning to end. The early stories are the most important and often the most negative. They cover major problems, typically national crises or political issues. Much of the newscast is then filled with more problem-focused content. The *last* story of the standard American network newscast is then positive. After roughly twenty-five minutes of bad news, the final story highlights something good: a major medical achievement, or a man who found his long-lost brother, or a home for lost pets.

Lest this seem like anecdotal evidence, let us reconsider some of the television data used in Figure 2. Many of the stories analyzed there do not include the order in which they appeared in a program – we know the show they appeared in and the date, but not the specific time. Data gathered after September 2018 for ABC show the precise time stories began, however.[6] We thus have nearly two years of evening ABC news stories with (a) a measure of valence and (b) the exact time the story aired.

Figure 4 plots the sentiment of more than three thousand ABC news stories, by minute, from 6:30 to 7:00 every evening from October 2018 to May 2020. The circles show estimates of valence for each story. The line shows the LOWESS-smoothed trend over the half-hour program. Note that 6:30 p.m. stories, those that come at the start of the broadcast, are on average the most negative. Stories in the last five minutes are in contrast markedly positive. Indeed, over the nineteen months analyzed here these stories are almost universally positive – only a dozen stories that begin after 6:55 p.m. have a net sentiment score below zero.

This phenomenon is not unique to ABC national news programs. We do not have access to as much data on other networks, but we did interview a number of journalists at Midwestern television stations.[7] Frederica Freyberg, executive producer of news and anchor of *Here and Now* for PBS Wisconsin, noted that in her time working in commercial news, "I actually never asked why, it just was."[8] A positive "kicker" in Freyberg's view is most common in commercial broadcasting and "designed to engender happy talk" between the anchor and reporters in an effort to build a connection between the anchor and the audience. "Also you don't want to leave the audience on a total downer before you say good night." Other television journalists echoed similar themes. Christina Lorey, a reporter and morning news show anchor at Channel 3 in Wisconsin, notes that "we like to leave viewers with a positive taste in their mouth, feeling a little hopeful, especially now with everything else going on."[9] (This last point, "especially now with everything else going on," is especially relevant to our discussion.)

---

[6] Data for CBS and NBC show only the start time of the episode – that is, 6:30 p.m. for all stories in a 6:30 p.m. show. ABC data include information on the precise time of the story prior to 2018 as well, but that information was not retrieved through the now-deprecated Web Services Kit. We are thus constrained here to the ABC data retrieved through the newer Lexis-Nexis Academic system.

[7] We are grateful to Michael Wagner for connecting us with these journalists.

[8] Frederica Freyberg was interviewed via telephone on October 23, 2020.

[9] Christina Lorey was interviewed via telephone on October 24, 2020.

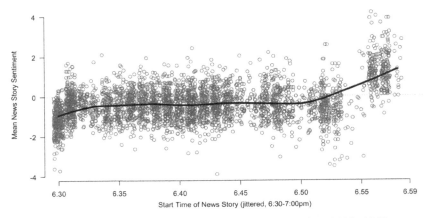

Figure 4 The valence of ABC evening news stories, 2018–2020

Circles show net sentiment for individual stories, based on 3,319 stories on *ABC World News Tonight* from October 2018 to May 2020. Lines show a LOWESS-smoothed average (f = 3). Sentiment is based on the LSD, as implemented in quanteda in R. Net sentiment is calculated as follows: log [(pos. counts + 0.5) / (neg. counts + 0.5)].

Indeed, Lorey reports shifting positive content to the beginning of the morning newscast as a way of shaking things up a little and finding a new audience. Alexandria Mack, producer at Milwaukee PBS, notes that "you want to leave viewers with some sort of optimism." Doing so during the pandemic reminds "people that we're all in this together"; it also means viewers are "more likely to watch again."[10] Matt Kummer, news director at WBAY in Green Bay, Wisconsin, spoke about the final story of a newscast as a "a way to leave people on a light-hearted note" and as something that has been "in the formula for TV news going back to its inception."[11] After the most important (and largely negative) headlines, the program finishes with "weather, sports, and a skiing squirrel."[12]

This phenomenon is also not unique to American news coverage. Qualitative assessments by international scholars suggest similar patterns in television news in Belgium, Canada, Germany, India, Italy, and Sweden.[13]

---

[10] Alexandria Mack was interviewed via telephone on October 26, 2020.

[11] Matt Kummer was interviewed via Zoom on October 23, 2020.

[12] We acknowledge that the skiing squirrel might be unique to Wisconsin news programming.

[13] We would not characterize this as a careful assessment of news coverage around the world – we mostly emailed trusted colleagues with expertise in communication, journalism, and/or politics. We are grateful to Jan van den Bulck, Bengt Johansson, Nojin Kwak, Amanda Lotz, Gianpietro Mazzoleni, Kenneth McElwain, Sriram Mohan, Elin Naurin, and Sven-Oliver Proksch for sharing their views of news programming elsewhere. Note also that the longer, later news programs in Germany do share this format, but the shorter (~20 minutes) prime-time newscasts do not. They are closer to the format of US local news, ending with sports and weather. The same

Those assessments also match the perceptions of journalists outside the United States. Susan Ritzén, news editor for major Swedish broadcaster SVT, noted that the final story of a broadcast is referred to as the *"rundisar,"* roughly translated as "round stuff."[14] Ritzén accounts for more positive content toward the end of a broadcast in several ways. There is a sense that a broadcast should as a whole present some kind of balance where valence is concerned.

> Maybe we don't think people would bother to watch unless we promise them something a bit more positive somewhere along the line. ... I think there is also a sense that the news anchor "leads" people through these mostly upsetting news segments, and that going from sad to very happy to sad would leave the viewer in an emotional roller coaster that could be confusing. ... But since our most "important" news [stories] are very serious and always presented first in a traditional linear news broadcast, the happier or lighter or brighter items therefore often end up at the end.

In short: *important* news is typically negative, so a change in pace (i.e., novelty) will tend to be positive.

The most telling comments from Ritzén were perhaps as follows: "During the corona pandemic we have a special item every day online where we gather positive news surrounding the coronavirus, like vaccine progress, survivors, countries where fewer become infected, and so on. Online this works very well; the positive news can also be placed on top of the web page. But unfortunately in traditional broadcast[s] they still tend to sink towards the end of the programme." We see two fascinating elements here. The first is that this balancing of positive and negative news is more easily achieved in an online news environment. (This is considered in much more detail in Section 3.3.) The second is that, in the midst of an especially negative news environment, positive news gets higher priority.

In sum, journalists' own accounts of news making make clear the perception that a half-hour broadcast should end with something a little different, a "rounding off" of what might otherwise be an exclusively negative newscast. This is not very different from what we have called novelty. After nearly

---

is true of South Korean newscasts. That said, sports and weather are clearly different from the "hard" news that makes up the bulk of the broadcast. Our expectation is that even a focus on sports and news toward the end of the broadcast would produce a trend in valence roughly similar to what we see in Figure 2. But regardless of whether valence changes, even news and weather are "something different" at the end of a newscast.

[14] Susan Ritzén was interviewed via email June 26–28, 2020.

a half hour of "regular" news content, people are ready for something less negative. Retaining an audience – either over the entire half hour or from one evening to the next – requires something a little different.[15]

3.1.3 Adaptive Processing

Turning to more positive content toward the end of a broadcast – or indeed at any point in our news-consuming behavior – may also be about adaptive processing. People often have to live through negative and stressful events. A global pandemic and racial injustice are psychologically difficult crises for people to process; so too are natural disasters and economic downturns. Although these types of events may initially seem overwhelming and all-encompassing, over time people turn to adaptive strategies. They attempt "to manage the demands created by stressful events that are appraised as taxing or exceeding a person's resources" (Taylor and Stanton 2007, p. 378). Put another way, even when faced with the unimaginable and the impossible, people try to adapt.

When people engage in adaptive processing, they are effectively taking in the state of the world and making it more manageable. Sometimes, this may mean searching for bigger meaning – that is, trying to make sense of a terrible tragedy (Gortner and Pennebaker 2003). Channeling anxiety into thinking about the welfare of others may also be part of this process (Gaspar et al. 2016). Other times, adapting may mean looking for a distraction, a piece of positive news during an otherwise bleak time (Skinner et al. 2003). Some people may adapt by simply tuning out (Skinner et al. 2003). Researchers identify many such adaptive techniques, and of course people can rely on different techniques at different points in time.

We can think of news valence as both a product of an outlet's goal to serve people's individual-level adaptive processing needs and a product of journalists engaging in adaptive processing themselves. Although initial coverage of a crisis may be overwhelmingly negative (indeed, reflecting the true negativity of a crisis), tasked with producing more and more content for an audience, the media may begin to search for stories that allow adaptive processing. Although negative coverage will still dominate, over time, stories may grow to include more positivity as the media try to help people make sense of the crisis. These

---

[15] This account also fits with explanations previously offered by those involved in news production (e.g., Steinberg 2018). On a nightly basis, viewers begin the newscast attentive to primarily negative news. A half hour later, bogged down by the negative content required to monitor the economy, the government, and the world, they are ready for something else.

types of more positive stories may even offer people a means of engaging in adaptive distraction strategies.

The events featured in Figure 2 – terrorism, school shootings, global pandemics, and racial injustice – are all psychologically difficult for people to process. The role of the news is not only to report on these events but also to make sense of them for a large, diverse audience (Gortner and Pennebaker 2003). This "sense-making" means moving forward, which may mean different types of stories. In the case of the COVID-19 pandemic, for example, it is reasonable to expect most of the news coverage to focus at first on the collective tragedy. Over time, however, more stories that highlight medical success or a supportive community will emerge. These more positive stories provide content that helps people make sense of the pandemic and adapt to their new reality. From a more strategic perspective, broadening the story content may also allow the news media to retain readers who may otherwise adapt to a crisis by disengaging from news entirely.

The journalists and editors putting together the news are also individuals trying to process a traumatic event. Just as news readers cannot sustain the constant negativity of a stressful crisis, so too this process may become overwhelming for news makers. Turning to at least somewhat more positive stories, then, is not only a strategy to retain readers, but also may help news makers themselves engage in adaptive processing.

In sum, the media may shift toward positive sentiment because this is how people work through crises: after an initial period of negativity, people start to make sense of a new reality and adapt.

Note that there are parallels between this adaptive processing argument and work that considers media use as a form of mood management (e.g., Moskalenko and Heine 2003; Zillmann 1988), life management (e.g., Hofer and Eden 2020), and coping more generally (for a review, see Wolfers and Schneider N.d.). Much of this work views media use in line with the classic "uses and gratifications" approach (Katz et al. 1973), which considers media consumption as a means of satisfying various psychological needs. There is in our view an important difference between the dynamic suggested in the literature on mood management and the literature on adaptive processing, however. In the former, media content is used to escape or enhance a mood and the subject matter of that media content can be anything at all – a sitcom, or drama, or sports, or news, etc. In adaptive processing, media coverage is typically viewed as a way of helping viewers process a specific event or situation, and the resulting positive content is thus more closely related (if not directly related) to that situation.

Escaping news about the pandemic almost certainly accounts for lots of entertainment viewing, for example, partly because we're all stuck at home, and partly as a way of coping with negative news content. The adaptive processing storyline suggests not just that we will seek out more positive content generally, however, but that we will also seek out more positive news *about the pandemic*. This is central to understanding why coverage of COVID shifts in a more positive direction so soon after the pandemic begins, and it fits with journalists' comments in Section 3.1.2 as well. A very negative event will tend to produce the need/demand for more positively valenced content about that event.

Regardless of whether attentiveness to positive content is about outlyingness, novelty, or adaptive processing, it is worth noting that *all* these accounts depend on news becoming very negative before there is sufficient demand for positive information. The system is self-correcting eventually, but it seems that there has to be a fair degree of negativity first. Waiting and hoping is not an especially attractive approach to shifting the valence of news coverage. But a greater concern is that even as these accounts suggest that demand for positive information will vary based on context, they do not suggest that there will be demand for positive information *at any given moment* in time. We believe that there is, however. The following section focuses on this possibility.

3.2 Valence-Based Asymmetries Vary across Individuals

Attentiveness to positive information is not contingent on context alone. At any given moment, in any given context, there will be individuals who are more interested in positive content than in negative content. On average, over time if not in the moment, humans will exhibit a negativity bias. But there is almost always a sizeable minority of individuals for whom positive content will be equally or more engaging.

Note that this is not an argument against prior findings that, on average, humans are more attentive to and activated by negative information. This is less a refutation of past work than a change in perspective. The average human exhibits a negativity bias in information processing – this fact is uncontested. But there is a great deal of variation around that average, and at any given time there will be an audience more interested in positive content than negative content, driven both by individual-level variation over both the short and long term, and by stable individual-level ("baseline") differences.

How big is that audience? This question is of some significance. If valence-based biases in information processing are such that a vast majority of the audience gravitates to negative information, then it makes sense for audience-seeking media to provide primarily negative content. Alternatively, if people who deliberately seek out news above any other type of content are more drawn to negative information, then it would also make sense for most news-related content to be negative.[16] If, on the other hand, a large minority is interested in positive news – both generally and among news seekers – then there may be both normative and financial reasons for media to offer more balanced content. We accordingly explore the distribution of valenced-based information biases in several ways here. We examine biases in news selection in new analyses of previously published data, first in a tightly controlled lab setting and then out there in the world (i.e., in *New York Times* reading habits). We then turn to psychophysiological experiments capturing activation by positive and negative television content. In each case, there is evidence of a considerable minority interested in positive rather than negative news.

We begin by reanalyzing data collected for Trussler and Soroka (2014). The data are from a lab experiment run in Montreal in 2012–2013. The main objective of the experiment was to explore whether respondents' stated preferences for positive or negative news matched their actual news consumption behavior. Since the researchers could not easily track respondents' news consumption habits at home, they designed a lab experiment in which respondents were told researchers were interested in tracking their eye movement while they watched a news video. To "tune" the eye-tracking camera, researchers first needed participants to read news on a website. Reading anything was fine, so long as they were reading. Participants were then presented with a mock news web page with headlines. They chose headlines to read, ostensibly unaware we were monitoring their choices. (Subjects were debriefed after the experiment, of course. Full details are available in Trussler and Soroka 2014.)

The aim of the original work was to compare news choices with stated preferences for news, captured in a survey toward the end of the experimental session. No significant links appeared between stated preferences and actual news-reading behavior: those who said they preferred more positive news chose predominantly negative headlines at the same rate as everyone else. This was predominantly true for campaign stories, at least; stories on policy did not show the same negativity bias. Here we focus on the campaign stories in which a negativity bias was most evident. Even in these stories, however, participants did not choose *exclusively* negative headlines. Figure 5 shows the likelihood of story selection based on the valence of headlines. The coauthors coded headlines and stories as positive, negative, or neutral. Three expert coders then coded every selection. There was unanimous agreement on codes in 86 percent of all cases; in the outlying cases, categorization was based on the majority decision.

---

[16] That said, few people either seek out only news (above other types of content) or fully avoid it (Prior 2005). Rather, most people fall between these two ends, varying in their news attention.

In Figure 5, we focus on the likelihood of headline selection across each of the three categories of valence.

A dotted horizontal line in Figure 5 indicates a likelihood of 1 – that is, the point at which headlines in a given category are selected at the same rate at which they are presented. Based on these experimental data, the likelihood of positive headlines being selected is roughly 0.74, the likelihood for neutral headlines is roughly 0.87, and the likelihood for negative headlines is roughly 1.27. Put differently, positive headlines are selected more than 20 percent *less* than they are presented, and negative headlines are selected more than 20 percent *more*.

A negativity bias in news selection is clear in Figure 5, then, but a large number of selected articles are neutral or positive nonetheless. Consider the following: if a news consumer is presented with a set of articles evenly split between the three categories, and if that consumer selects stories at the rates shown in Figure 5, then the chosen set of stories would still be roughly 26 percent positive. Even when negative biases are present, there still is at least some attentiveness to positive news.

There are reasons to expect news selection in a strange lab environment to differ from news selection in the "real world." It is, however, possible to see the same basic dynamic in observational data as well. Figure 6 shows the distribution of articles that made the top ten most viewed articles daily in the *New York*

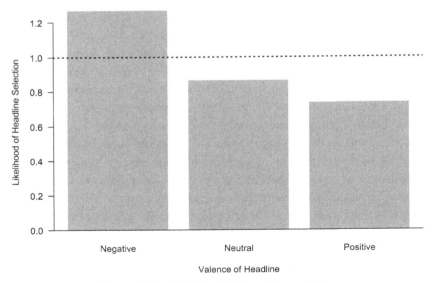

Figure 5 The likelihood of headline selection

Data from Trussler and Soroka (2014). Based on the frequency with which participants selected negative, neutral, and positive headlines.

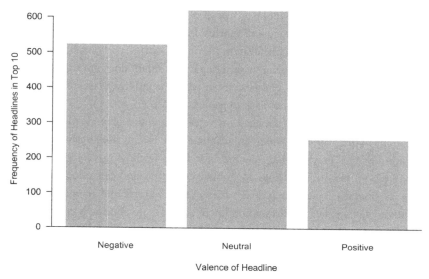

Figure 6 The valence of the top-ten viewed articles in the *New York Times*
Data from Kraft et al. (2020). Sentiment is based on the LSD, as implemented in
quanteda in R.

Times from February 18 to April 28, 2015. The data are drawn from recent work
by Kraft et al. (2020), focused on differences in the valence of articles that are
viewed versus those that are recirculated via Facebook, Twitter, and email. The
crux of the paper is as follows. Given the nature of sharing information across
different platforms, the authors argue that the distribution of valence in shared
stories should be more positive than the distribution of valence for read stories.
They examine this by comparing the valence of all stories on top-ten lists over
the roughly ten-week period. The original findings focus on shifting distributions of an interval-level measure of valence, based on automated content
analysis of articles using the LSD. (This is the same approach used for the
data in Figures 1 and 2.) Here we categorize stories into three categories in order
to produce data roughly similar to what we have seen in Figure 5. Stories in
which negative words outnumber positive words are categorized as negative,
stories in which positive words outnumber negative words are categorized as
positive, and other stories are categorized as neutral. Figure 6 shows the
distribution of valence in articles *New York Times* readers chose to view.

As in Figure 5, the *New York Times* data in Figure 6 exhibit a negativity bias.
There are a good number of neutral headlines – 44 percent of headlines are by
this categorization not clearly negative or positive. The proportion of clearly
negative headlines outweighs the proportion of clearly positive headlines by

a factor of 2 (37 percent versus 18 percent). That said, roughly one in five headlines for the top-ten viewed stories in the *New York Times* is clearly positive, and three in five headlines for those stories are either neutral or positive. Again, the inclination toward negative content does not translate into exclusively negative news choices. Even when negativity biases are present, there is at least some attentiveness to positive news.

Taken together, results from headline selections in the lab and from headline selections in the *New York Times* suggest that there is a non-negligible audience for not-negative news. What accounts for these findings given the sizeable literatures on negativity biases in human cognition and behavior? In short, even as humans exhibit negativity biases in reactions and attentiveness to negative versus positive information, there is at any given time a great deal of variation around that mean. This fact is illustrated in a rather different way in Figure 7, which shows the distribution of participant negativity biases in activation from psychophysiological experiments conducted in the United States, Canada, and the UK.

Data in Figure 7 are drawn from Soroka et al. (2019) and Fournier et al. (2020). The original sample includes results from seventeen countries; here we

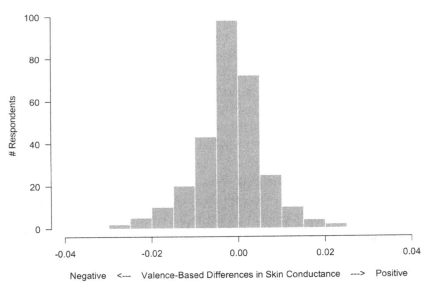

Figure 7 Reactions to positive versus negative video news content

Data from Soroka et al. (2019). Differences in skin conductance are coefficients capturing participants' reactivity to positive versus negative content over the course of seven BBC news stories. Based on 403 participants from the United States, Canada, and the UK.

reduce heterogeneity in the sample somewhat by focusing on three Anglo-American countries.[17] The histogram shows the distribution of "valence-based differences in skin conductance," estimated as follows. Respondents sit down in front of a laptop computer, with sensors attached to their fingers, to watch seven BBC news stories. Five of the seven stories are randomly drawn from a sample of four positive international stories and four negative international stories. The remaining two stories are about the local country, one positive and one negative. Stories are randomly ordered and coded second by second for valence by multiple human coders. (Full details on the coding of valence is available in Soroka et al. 2019.)

For each respondent, then, we have a time series of second-by-second valence in news content, and second-by-second skin conductance levels. Skin conductance – essentially a measure of how much a respondent is sweating – is a standard psychophysiological measure of activation in the sympathetic ("fight-or-flight") nervous system. When respondents are not excited or bored, skin conductance tends to be low; when they are activated and interested, skin conductance tends to be comparatively high. By using a time-series model in which skin conductance is regressed on the tone of video content, we can estimate a coefficient capturing, for each individual, the average difference in skin conductance that is the product of a one-unit increase in news valence.[18]

Figure 7 shows the distribution of these coefficients across all 403 participants. Negative values indicate individuals who exhibit more psychophysiological activation in response to negative news content. Positive values indicate individuals who exhibit more psychophysiological activation in response to positive news content. The average, in line with the existing literature, suggests a negativity bias. (The average for the data shown in Figure 6 is −0.002, which is statistically different from zero at $p < 0.001$.) But a sizeable minority of respondents clearly exhibit positivity rather than negativity biases. Twenty-five percent of respondents in these Anglo-American countries have a coefficient above +0.002 – significantly different from zero and *positive* rather than negative.

To what extent does the variation in Figure 7 reflect "real" variation around the mean rather than random noise? It is certainly possible that the variation we see in Figure 7 is less about individual-level differences in information processing, and more the product of random error in the measurement and/or modeling of physiological activation. Indeed, the same might be said for the measurement of valence in news content in Figures 5 and 6 – in these cases too, either the

---

[17] Results are the same when the entire sample is used, however; see Soroka et al. (2019).

[18] We do not go into detail here on the methods used to smooth and "normalize" skin conductance, but note that all information is available in both Soroka et al. (2019) and Fournier et al. (2020).

automated content-analytic method or random error in the measure of human behavior may produce a distribution that is less clearly negative than if these quantities were measured without error. There are good reasons to believe that the variation both in viewed news content and physiological activation is real, however. A considerable body of literature after all demonstrates stable valence-based differences in learning. Some individuals learn more from positive information, while others learn more from negative information (e.g., Fazio et al. 2004). The latter group is somewhat larger, as we might expect. But there is variation, and most important for our purposes, that variation is linked to news consumption as well (Bachleda et al. 2020; Soroka et al. N.d.).

Moreover, as the preceding sections on outlyingness, novelty, and adaptive processing have suggested, even individuals who exhibit negativity biases on average will in certain contexts be less inclined toward negative information. The end of a half-hour news broadcast may be one of those times, and so might any context in which news has been so sufficiently and systematically negative that positive content becomes outlying. The proportion of news consumers interested in positive content (maybe one quarter of news consumers, based on results in Figures 5 through 7) needn't be the same group of people all the time. Stable individual-level differences arise in valence-based biases, and context-dependent differences occur as well. As a result, some individuals are more likely to find themselves on the positive end of Figure 7 most of the time, but many individuals may find themselves there at one point or another.

To what extent can we distinguish between the different individuals who may end up more likely to find themselves leaning toward negative or positive information? Section 3.1 has offered ample evidence of time-varying (or state-based) differences in valence-based asymmetries. The present section has offered only limited evidence for durable (or trait-based) differences, however. What we *do* know based on the existing evidence is that at any given point in time there are differences in humans' negativity or positivity biases. This is the critical part of our argument – that is, we need both over-time and cross-sectional variation in preferences for positive or negative information. The extent to which this cross-sectional variation reflects durable individual-level differences, however, is unclear. We can point to recent work that finds a correlation in the same individuals' preferences for negative headlines at two different points in time (Bachleda et al. 2020), or work connecting (ostensibly durable) learning biases to news consumption (Soroka et al. N.d.). There also is a considerable body of work arguing that certain types of negativity biases are related to political conservatism (Hibbing et al. 2014; Shook and Fazio 2009) – a finding that could be interpreted to suggest, at least indirectly, that individuals have durable valence-based asymmetries. Recent research, however, finds no such ideological differences (Bakker et al. 2020; Fournier et al. 2020). Moreover, durable trait differences in valence-based asymmetries are not evidenced by any single study finding cross-sectional variation, even if this variation happens to correlate with other traits scholars believe to be relatively stable.

Regardless of whether valence-based biases are primarily a state- or a trait-level difference, it nevertheless seems very likely, given the available evidence, that most people do at some point look for positive rather than negative news. The inclination to seek out positive information needn't be a conscious one; our attentiveness to positive rather than negative information may be entirely unconscious, driven by what we've seen in the recent past or by the distribution of information we have accumulated over an extended period. But this inclination can be conscious as well. Indeed, these types of decisions and behaviors are part of individuals' adaptive processes. Confronted with a crisis – or even a particularly bad day – people gravitate toward information that will help them deal with the negativity around them. Certainly, for some people this may mean seeking out more information about a crisis, but for others this will mean searching for more positive content as a means of easing the stress.

When everything seems negative, we can, at the end of a news broadcast, look forward to the positive story that experience tells us comes just before the half hour is up. We can decide to page down on the *Washington Post* website to reach the "Lifestyle" or "Arts & Entertainment" sections. We can also close the *Washington Post* website entirely and open up Instagram for a more reliable dose of positive content.

Moving from a traditional news source like the *Washington Post* to a new source like Instagram strikes us as an especially interesting possibility. Traditional media have always produced at least a modicum of positively valenced coverage, but new digital media may produce a rather different distribution of news content (Soroka et al. 2017). Moreover, changes in the media landscape may produce more readily accessible positive content. This is the focus of the next section.

3.3 Technology Facilitates Diverse News Platforms Catering to Diverse Preferences

Establishing heterogeneity in preferences for negative information is not enough to sustain the argument that there is an increasing viability of positive news. That argument requires one more step: a demonstration that, in light of variability in news consumers' valence-based biases in information processing, the changing media environment is likely to produce more positive content.

3.3.1 An Increasing Number of Media Outlets Facilitates More Diverse Content

A considerable body of work suggests that increasing numbers of media outlets tend to produce a more diverse distribution of content. We do not present new data on this possibility here – the extant literature contains ample evidence. We consider some examples.

The argument that increased sources tends to produce diversity in content predates the current digital era. Indeed, much of the evidence comes from observing shifts in newspaper and television markets, particularly the latter given the Federal Communication Commission's (like many other agencies in other countries) long-standing effort to encourage diversity in broadcasting (see, e.g., Glasser 1984; Roessler 2007). Findings vary based on the measures used to capture "diversity," focusing, for instance, on diversity in source, content, and exposure diversity (Napoli 1999; also see Hellman 2001). The balance of evidence in both radio (e.g., Chambers 2003) and television (e.g., Aslama et al. 2004; Grant 1994; De Jong and Bates 1991) nevertheless points in the direction of increasing program diversity with an increasing number of competitors – albeit with some limitations, including decreasing program diversity alongside ownership concentration.

The Internet clearly offers ready access to innumerable audiences, from very broad to very targeted, and a low bar of entry for those interested in disseminating news content. It is of course still the case that online news is dominated by large media agencies, some traditional and some digital; ownership concentration is accordingly still a concern (e.g., Vizcarrondo 2013). There is nevertheless evidence that the online news environment presents citizens with increasingly diverse content. Powers and Benson (2014) find increasing diversity in genres, topics and authors in US news media, with more mixed results in France and Denmark. Humprecht and Esser (2018) find that diversity in online news platforms is more likely in markets with strong public service media (a finding that is similar for offline news platforms as well), but there is a lot of variation across both markets and mediums. Where the United States is concerned, Powers and Benson note that "online, U.S. news outlets exhibit as much – and in some cases more – overall diversity and cross-outlet deviation as their European counterparts" (p. 259).

The existence of diversity and audiences' exposure to it are of course two different things (Napoli 1997). This fact is central to Prior's (2007) foundational work detailing the ways in which the expansion of cable television facilitated more content, but also citizens' ability to opt entirely out of current affairs–focused content. A high-choice online media environment may thus offer a lot of content diversity while simultaneously allowing audiences to select very little content diversity. This concern has of course been considered in great detail in the literature on selective exposure (e.g., Stroud 2011). The decision to "select" into different kinds of information will be central to our argument. For now, however, we concentrate on the *provision* of diverse content. In this regard, there are good reasons to believe that the online environment is advantageous.

Our perspective on the future of online news content is informed by this existing literature on content diversity and market competition, alongside our preceding findings on diversity in psychophysiological reactions to news content. Audience-seeking journalism has for a long time aimed news content at the average news consumer. That average consumer is, most of the time, more attentive to negative news. When news outlets are limited in number and in their ability to "target" their news content to individuals' preferences, and thus fighting over the same potential audience, then it makes sense that news content will be targeted toward that average consumer. In the 1980s, for instance, it makes sense that ABC, CBS, and NBC produce newscasts that follow a similar storyline, focused mainly on negative news with a "rounding off" moment at the end. This is in all likelihood what the average viewer is interested in. The same is true for network evening television broadcasts now. But technological change has shifted fundamentally the ways in which audiences can select content online, and thus the ways in which news producers make content. Diverse content and diverse preferences combine to make for a much more flexible news environment, in terms both of production and of consumption.

3.3.2 Online Affordances Augment Valence-Based Selectivity

An increasing number of television stations (and wireless television remotes) produced a television-viewing environment in which changing channels was increasingly easy and attractive. The shift toward time-shifted programming on Netflix and elsewhere created a viewing experience that is even more in the audience's control. The evolving flexibility of our television experience pales in comparison to the control we have over content on a computer or smartphone, however. At every click we make a programming decision. What we can click on is in large part still under the control of news producers. But when one site (or smartphone app) does not have the content we want, we can simply click somewhere else.

Whether this media environment produces more or less diversity from a single news producer is (to us) as yet unclear. We can imagine two possibilities. One is that a news producer, leveraging the now unlimited online "space" for content, will try to provide very broadly diverse content. Different people will be interested in different things at different times, and perhaps all of those things can be found on a single site. At the same time, news producers, facing increasing competition and a need to attract a stable audience, may specialize. The Internet already makes it straightforward for a small organization to reach a small but geographically dispersed membership. Where news providers are concerned, this ability to specialize and thus to reach a dispersed but sufficient audience may be similarly advantageous.[19] Where positively valenced content is concerned, even if a minority of individuals are interested in positive content at any given time, it is feasible for news providers to produce content for and to reach that audience.

Do news providers produce and reach audiences interested in positively valenced content? We explore this question by focusing on a database of news agencies' Facebook posts, gathered by Dan Hiaeshutter-Rice. (See Hiaeshutter-Rice and Weeks N.d. and Hiaeshutter-Rice 2020.) The database goes back nearly to the beginning of Facebook and continues to early 2017 (when the Facebook API changed and downloading public posts became more difficult). The corpus itself includes all posts from the roughly five hundred top-shared public affairs–oriented public pages on Facebook. This includes most major news agencies, alongside a good number of fringe news outlets. The total number of posts in this Facebook database is more than 13 million.

We begin by looking at the overall relationship between the valence of Facebook news posts and the number of "shares" those posts receive. We focus on posts from calendar years 2011 to 2016, since before this time news agencies were less systematically posting on Facebook. We estimate the valence of the text across all 13 million Facebook posts using the LSD. We then estimate a simple bivariate regression model where the total number of shares is a function of the valence of a post. Since our dependent variable is a count variable, we use a Poisson regression model. Results of that model are shown in Table 1.

The findings in Table 1 should come as no surprise given what we have seen: positively valenced posts receive fewer shares on Facebook. (This is evidenced by the negative coefficient for valence.) Looking across a massive sample of posts, there is a negativity bias in the sharing of news posts on Facebook. A considerable literature on negativity biases suggests that this should be the finding *on average*, of course, but our discussion suggests that we should expect a good deal of variation around this average. Here we explore that variation with an eye on differences across news outlets that tend to emphasize negatively or positively valenced content.

---

[19] For an early discussion focused on newspapers, see Carroll (1985).

Table 1 The impact of valence on Facebook shares

Cells contain coefficients from Poisson regression models with standard errors in parentheses. * p < 0.01. Based on all posts from 2011 to 2016 across ~450 top recirculated news outlets. Higher valence values mean more positive valence.

	Dependent Variable: Number of Facebook Shares
Valence	−0.029*
	(0.000)
Constant	4.969*
	(0.000)
N	12,689,551

* p < 0.05. *Valence* takes on values above and below zero, where increasing values indicate more positive valence.

We do not have priors about the average valence of posts from all Facebook sites, of course, but there are well-known outlets that focus on negative or positive information. Figure 8 shows the distribution of positive, neutral, and negative valence across eight such outlets. Outlets in the left column tend to emphasize negative content. The mean valence of *Breitbart* posts is more negative than the overall mean, but the distribution of *Breitbart* content over this time period actually leans only slightly toward the negative, at least in comparison with the other outlets in the left column of Figure 8. *Freedom Daily News* and *Controversial Times* are well-known and predominantly negative conservative outlets. *Media Matters* is a well-known and predominantly negative liberal outlet. And to be clear, this is by no means a random sample of negative outlets – it is just a handpicked set of four that we know to be predominantly negative.

The same is true for the positively inclined outlets in the right column of Figure 8. *The Huffington Post* is a special case – it is by far the largest outlet examined here, and although it is not expressly focused on positive content, Arianna Huffington did note publicly in 2015 that this outlet would try to concentrate more on positive content. (She cited the tendency of readers to recirculate positive stories more, which we test directly here.) *Upworthy*, in contrast, is an expressly positive (and liberal) outlet. *The Barracuda Brigade* and *Occupy Democrats* are mobilization/participation-focused outlets focused on conservatives and liberals, respectively. Note that the former is more positive than many well-known conservative sites, although its posts lean only marginally toward positive.

The purpose of Figure 8 is twofold. First, results demonstrate significant differences in the valence of posts by different news outlets. Some tend to post negative content; others tend to post positive content. Having said that, even

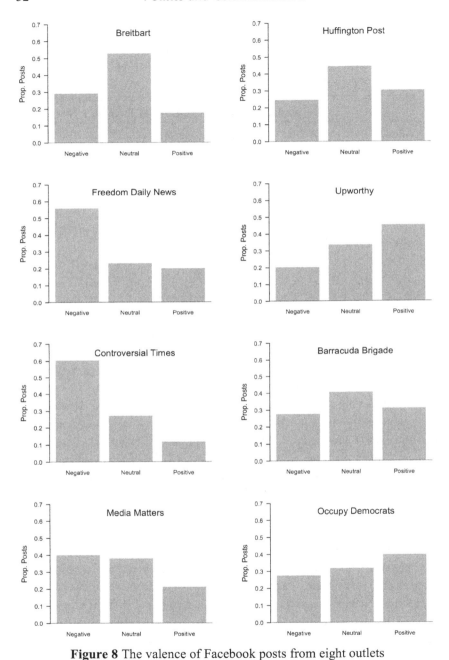

Figure 8 The valence of Facebook posts from eight outlets

Data from Hiaeshutter-Rice (2020) Valence is estimated using the LSD. Based on all posts from each outlet from 2011 to 2016.

within each outlet there is some diversity in valence. Even in the *Controversial Times*, easily the most negative outlet amongst this set (and amongst the most negative of *all* outlets, based on diagnostic tests), roughly 10 percent of posts are positive and 25 percent are neutral. This within-source variation is of real importance for our next set of analyses, which focuses on the impact of valence on shares *within* each of these eight sources.

In Tables 2 and 3, we explore the possibility that each valence-focused outlet has a corresponding valence-focused audience – more specifically, that negatively valenced (/positively valenced) outlets will attract audiences that are particularly interested in negatively valenced (/positively valenced) content, where "interest" will be captured here using Facebook shares. Our hypothesis is that negative outlets will receive more shares for posts that are more negative, and positive outlets will receive more share for posts that are positive.

The hypothesis is clearly supported by results in Tables 2 and 3. The coefficient for valence is negative in each case in Table 2, indicating that positive valence is *negatively* associated with shares. Note that the direction of these coefficients is as we saw in the general model in Table 1, but the magnitude of each of these coefficients is far larger. The negativity bias seen in Facebook shares generally in Table 1 is strengthened when we focus on the negative outlets in Table 2. Table 3 completes the picture by modeling sharing behavior from the four outlets with an expressed inclination toward positive content. Note that the coefficients for valence in Table 3 are all positive. In each of these outlets, positive valence is associated with *more* shares.

Table 2 The negative impact of valence on Facebook shares

Cells contain coefficients from Poisson regression models with standard errors in parentheses. *p < 0.01. Based on all posts from 2011 to 2016 from the following sources:

(1) Breitbart (generally negative conservative outlet)
(2) Freedom Daily News (generally negative conservative outlet)
(3) Controversial Times (generally negative conservative outlet)
(4) Media Matters (generally negative liberal outlet)

	Dependent Variable: Number of Facebook Shares			
	1	2	3	4
Valence	−0.189*	−0.055*	−0.187*	−0.053*
	(0.000)	(0.000)	(0.016)	(0.000)
Constant	6.931*	6.454*	1.210*	5.810*
	(0.000)	(0.000)	(0.020)	(0.000)
N	40,904	25,880	1,253	19,004

Table 3 The positive impact of valence on Facebook shares

Cells contain coefficients from Poisson regression models with standard errors in parentheses. * p < 0.01. Based on all posts from 2011 to 2016 from the following sources:

(1) Huffington Post (news with a stated commitment to more positive content)
(2) Upworthy (obviously positive)
(3) Barracuda Brigade (generally positive, participation-focused conservative outlet)
(4) Occupy Democrats (generally positive, participation-focused liberal outlet)

	Dependent Variable: Number of Facebook Shares			
	1	2	3	4
Valence	0.028*	0.094*	0.421*	0.215*
	(0.000)	(0.000)	(0.000)	(0.000)
Constant	6.452*	7.718*	3.981*	8.904*
	(0.000)	(0.000)	(0.000)	(0.000)
N	97,056	20,692	135,680	25,759

The eight sources used in Tables 2 and 3 are not meant as a representative sample of Facebook sites – they are intended only as an illustration of the fact that sharing behavior can vary by site, in some cases in line with the valence-based bias of the news source. That said, they do make clear that in spite of the average negativity bias, there are at least some news providers for whom positive content reaches a broader audience. This is exactly as we expect. In sum, online news allows for much more content from a wide array of providers given diverse audience interests. There consequently may be advantages to specializing and building an audience for certain types of content; some news producers specialize in positively or negatively valenced content, and those outlets have audiences with sharing preferences in line with the outlets' valence-based priorities.

That the online news environment augments selectivity in news content is not a new claim, of course. That it augments selectivity in news consumption based on the valence of that content is, perhaps. It is, however, worth noting that our argument here parallels work exploring valence-based homophily in social networks. The strength of Twitter network connections about political issues appears to be partly based on the typical valence of users' posts, for instance – above and beyond their political ideology (Himelboim et al. 2016). Some Twitter users have posts and networks that are predominantly negatively valenced; others have posts and networks that are predominantly positively valenced, ceteris paribus. Similar evidence of emotional homophily has been found on MySpace (Thelwall 2010), Weibo (Song et al. 2016), and YouTube (Rosenbusch et al. 2019).[20] In each case, the strength of personal connections or networks appears to be premised at least in part on users' tendencies to be attracted to and/or recirculate information with a particular emotion or valence.

Given this behavior on social media, it seems entirely possible that as we learn about the valence of information on various news sites we might adjust our news-consumption behavior, actively and effectively seeking out positive or negative information. We accordingly take the preceding results for Facebook shares as (admittedly partial) evidence that news consumers engage in selectivity where the valence of information is concerned. This behavior should be more prevalent in an increasingly high-choice digital news environment.

3.3.3 Information consumption and (re-)distribution in a hybrid media environment

Technological change has produced an increasing number of news outlets and facilitated an audience-generating strategy that may well reward specialization in positively rather than negatively valenced content. This is because humans' interest in positive information will vary both across individuals and over time, and there is regularly a sizeable minority (if not a majority) of individuals interested in positively valenced news content. As the preceding section has shown, there also is reason to believe that news consumers learn where to go for news that is positively valenced. To what extent can we be sure that individuals actually move between different news sources based on valence, however?

In order for any one person to practice valence-based news searching they first must have ready access to news content with varying valences, within a single source or across multiple sources. Within-source variability will certainly exist much of the time in most major news outlets. We have already seen that television news content provides a predictable combination of negative and positive content, after all. Most newspapers will offer the same balance of positive and negative news, as will most major news outlets online. Selecting content that suits our valence-based preference often requires no more than clicking on a different section or story.

But to fully appreciate the ways which people move between differently valenced information streams both online and offline we need to consider how information consumption works in a "hybrid media system" (Chadwick 2013). Chadwick argues that a hybrid media system is one in which traditional and "new" news agencies, individuals, bloggers, social media users and many others

---

Relatedly, news sites are more likely to link to other news content when is has a similar valence (Turetsky and Riddle 2018).

all interact, with differing but also overlapping (and conflated) logics. We characterize the part of Chadwick's argument most relevant to our work as follows. The movement of information in a hybrid system is not *between* sources/actors so much as *amongst* all of them. A political campaign or major event occurs as a combination of interactions from multiple actors, both anticipating and reacting to information from other actors. And political information is increasingly conceived of with this hybridity in mind.[21] We have a similar view of news consumption. Individuals increasingly select and consume news content with the understanding that their experience will reflect some combination of topics, perspectives, and valences, curated moment-to-moment through clicks across multiple buttons, remotes, screens and/or apps. In this way, information consumption is increasingly hybrid.

Demonstrating this directly is of course complex. "Digital trace data" (e.g., Jungherr 2015) offers perhaps the best opportunity to explore the nature of information selection and consumption in real time, but even these data cannot capture everything that comes across our screen (they typically capture only things we click on); nor can they capture information seeking across a combination of mobile phones, televisions, and newsprint. There nevertheless are survey data that get at least in part at the behaviors we are interested in examining. We turn to some of those data here.

We consider first some data from an early 2015 survey (N = 1,046) from the American Press Institute and the Associated Press-NORC Center for Public Affairs Research.[22] The survey has limited information about the specific outlets and topics which respondents consider each day, but it does have two questions capturing variation in both the number of "technologies" and the number "sources" that respondents use. Six different technologies are listed, including, e.g., television, radio, computers. Eight different sources are listed, including, e.g., local TV, network TV, and online-only news sources. The complete lest of technologies and sources is included in the notes to Figure 9.

The figure itself shows the distribution of respondents selected between one and six technologies and between one and eight sources. Histograms for each variable are shown on the top and to the right of the graphic. The main panel shows (jittered) circles for each respondent. There is a clear relationship

---

[21] There is perhaps a danger in putting too much emphasis on the hybridity of the current media system. There are still differences between news sources and technological platforms, of course, and both news producers and news consumers are well aware of these. (See, e.g., Hiaeshutter-Rice 2020) But the notion that information production increasingly occurs with the interactions of a hybrid media system in mind rings true.

[22] This is an RDD sample conducted by a third-party vendor, Marketing Systems Group. The final response rate was 23 percent based on the Council of American Survey Research Organizations method.

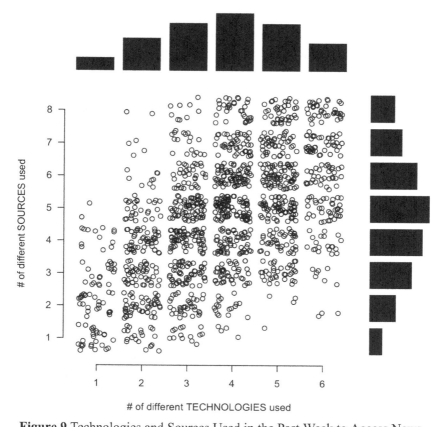

Figure 9 Technologies and Sources Used in the Past Week to Access News.

Data from The Associated Press-NORC Center for Public Affairs Research, The Personal News Cycle, March 2015. The six different TECHNOLOGIES recorded here are: (1) television, (2) radio, (3) print newspapers or magazines, (4) computers, (5) mobile phones, and (6) other screens combined (including tablets, e-readers and smart TVs). The eight different SOURCES recorded here are: (1) local TV, (2) network TV, (3) cable TV, (4) radio, (5) newspapers (paper or otherwise), (6) magazines (paper or otherwise), (7) online-only news sources (e.g., Yahoo, Huffington Post), and newswires (e.g., AP).

between increasing sources and increasing technologies, of course. But the finding that we want to highlight most in Figure 9 is that the modal respondent relies on five sources across four technologies. People regularly get information from many different places.

Figure 9 is just a starting point for an argument about news consumption in the new media system. In this media system where people rely on multiple technologies and sources, how exactly do they choose where to get their information? Imagine two possibilities. In the first, respondents rely on multiple sources (as we have seen in Figure 9) but use all sources for roughly similar, overlapping kinds of information. In the second, a variety of known options creates a context in which people can purposefully turn to certain outlets for certain types of news – in particular, they turn to some outlets for positive news, as a way of counter-balancing the negative information they receive from other outlets.

Put differently: in the first instance, a person may visit Twitter as their chief source of information about politics, sports, and entertainment – assuming that the social media platform will provide enough of all of these. In this case, if much of the information on a given day on Twitter is negative, much of the information this person receives will also be negative. In the second instance, a person may visit Twitter to keep abreast of the latest information, but also visit Instagram because the environment there is likely more positive. (We consider this possibility in particular below.) The goal of visiting Instagram for this person is to ensure that positive information enters their day in some form.

We cannot easily observe this valence-based outlet-switching behavior directly. We can nevertheless look further into how people construct their news and information environments. We rely here on a survey ($N = 1,046$) conducted in the winter of 2015 by the Media Insight Project and the Associated Press-NORC (AP-NORC) Center. The goal of the survey was to consider the media habits of "millennials" – defined here as people between the ages of eighteen and thirty-four at the time of the survey.[23]

What is particularly beneficial about the survey for our purposes are the detailed questions about the intersection of topic and source. Participants were given a series of topics such as celebrities and pop culture, sports, the arts, health, and general news; in total, participants were asked about eight different topics. They were then asked which outlets they use to follow information about a particular topic – assuming they followed a particular topic at all. The outlets ranged from social media sites like Facebook or Twitter, news outlets like newspapers or news aggregators, and other types of outlets like blogs and entertainment websites.

We can use this series of questions to track patterns in the use of outlets and the extent to which people deliberately diversify how they get information. To do so, we can rely on the following simple calculation:

$$\frac{\text{\# of topics followed with source}}{\text{\# of total topics followed}} \times 100$$

---

[23] The American Association for Public Opinion Research (AAPOR) Response Rate 3 for the survey was 14 percent; the survey was conducted on the Web.

This calculation provides the percentage of topics for which a respondent uses the same source – it is a measure of variation in the use of informational sources. A result close to 100 percent suggests that respondents are generally indiscriminate in their use of a source – that is, they use that source for information on *all* the topics they follow. Smaller values suggest more selective use – that is, respondents use that source only for selected topics. We calculate this measure for each of the outlets included in the survey and present the results by source in Table 4.

The results presented in Table 4 suggest significant variation in the use of sources. Only one source, Facebook, is used for (just barely) more than half of the topics respondents follow. The vast majority of sources are used for less than a quarter (less than two of eight) of the topics respondents follow. This finding is in line with our expectation that people seek out particular kinds of information from particular sources.

Figure 9 shows that people use multiple sources and technologies; Table 4 demonstrates that they use these sources for different things. These findings are squarely in line with our expectation that people purposefully move between outlets to find the information they are interested in. One source of interest or attentiveness is, we argue, information that is likely to have a valence in line

Table 4 The percentage of topics respondents follow, by source

Cells show the percentage of topics for which a respondent uses each source. Data are from the 2015 survey by the Media Insight Project and the AP-NORC.

	Mean	SE
Facebook	55.14%	1.34%
Search Engine	42.99%	1.26%
Word of Mouth	40.57%	1.30%
Other Social Media	25.04%	1.06%
National TV	24.58%	1.02%
Local TV	24.36%	1.02%
Media Focuses on One Topic	22.67%	1.00%
Radio	21.61%	0.97%
Online-Only Publisher	19.79%	0.99%
Blog	16.01%	0.91%
Twitter	14.20%	0.97%
Local Newspaper	13.91%	0.83%
Online Aggregator	13.59%	0.88%
National Newspaper	9.21%	0.70%

with our valence-based preference. This last component of our argument is not clearly demonstrated by these survey-based findings; it is, however, in line with them. And we believe that we can make the case for purposeful valence-based information seeking through a more qualitative account.

3.3.4 Deliberately Seeking Good News

That people rely on one source to follow sports but a different source to follow the local art scene is in some ways to be expected. In an environment where outlets must compete for attention, it makes sense that outlets would work to develop competitive advantages in specific content areas. Moreover, people may develop their own informational habits by relying on the same outlets time after time.

More notable, perhaps, is the possibility that certain outlets will deliberately work to attract and retain audiences by creating an environment of positivity. These outlets capitalize on people's desire for positive information. People may be interested in, follow, and share negative news, but they may also turn to other outlets specifically to block out (if even artificially) the negativity. One such current beacon of positivity is Instagram.

Because Instagram is primarily a visual platform featuring images that can include only limited captions, the focus is on the images' aesthetic impact. The result, researchers have suggested, is a medium concentrated on sharing positive content (Sheldon and Bryant 2016; Waterloo et al. 2018). Reflecting this positivity, Waterloo et al. (2018) found that people believed that Instagram was the *least* appropriate platform (relative to Facebook, Twitter, and WhatsApp) for expressing sadness, anger, and disappointment – all negative emotions. Instagram is, as the *New York Times* described it, "a simple, staged stream of positivity" – a place without "heavy news stories" (Victor 2018).

People are generally unlikely to turn to Instagram for a dose of politics. In the 2019 fall wave of Pew's American Trend's Panel, for example, respondents were asked to report which social media platforms they use to obtain political news. Of those who had heard about Instagram (about 86 percent of the sample), only 7.5 percent reported that they would use the platform for political news – compared to 27 percent who reported they would use Facebook and 15.4 percent who reported they would use Twitter.

Instagram may not be a source for political news, but it is not free of politics. In 2016, for example, political candidates made use of the platform by offering "polished images" of their campaign events and rallies and linking campaign information from their profiles (Bossetta 2018). As one may expect, people who are interested in politics are also drawn to following these political figures on

Instagram (much as they would be drawn to following politics on Twitter and Facebook; Parmelee and Roman 2019). But even here Instagram offers a *different* kind of politics:

> Political news as delivered by newspapers and television can be so negative that the respondents may actively seek alternative information platforms, such as Instagram, to get a more light-hearted take on the current political environment. . . . As a result, political leaders have an interest in including at least some entertaining posts in their feed. (Parmelee and Roman 2019, 9)

In an environment of negativity, then, people deliberately rely on (and contribute to) Instagram as a mainly positive platform.[24] This is notable. The idea that people deliberately seek out Instagram in order to interact more positively with the world – even when it comes to politics – suggests a clear and steady desire for positively valenced content. And while Instagram may be the paradigmatic example, it is not the only one. As we have seen, some Facebook sites are known for positive content, and an increasing number of news outlets well beyond Facebook focus on more positively valenced content. Positive news need not be restricted to the last five minutes of the evening newscast or the bottom of a news website. By making individuals' varying preferences for content more actionable, technological change is leading to a fundamentally different news information environment.

4 Discussion

Our argument is that valence-based biases in information processing vary across individuals and time, and that technology increasingly facilitates a news environment catering to diverse valence-based interests. The result of these processes is that positively valenced stories will surface even when the news context is predominantly negative.

We believe that this argument helps account for the findings in Figures 1 and 2. Recall that Figure 1 demonstrated a shift toward more positively valenced newspaper content only weeks after the beginning of the COVID-19 pandemic and the 2020 BLM movement. Figure 2 then found that the tone of television news content – contrary to what many observers might suspect – has *not* become more negatively valenced over time. We regard both dynamics – positive shifts in the coverage of objectively negative events, and a steady equilibrium in the valence of television news content over the past thirty years – as the product of

---

[24] This positivity is not without negative externalities. For instance, the "Instagram culture" has allowed certain conspiracy theories to thrive because they are nestled in beautifully packaged images and surrounded by positive comments (Tiffany 2020).

partly stable and partly time-varying individual-level differences in valence-based information processing.

Humans do regularly exhibit negativity biases in information processing. This is a well-established fact, and it is as evident in news selection as in any number of other information-gathering behaviors. But a good deal of variation exists around average human behavior, driven by a focus on outlyingness or novelty in the context of changing information environments, or by the need for adaptive processing in response to negative events, or by durable individual-level differences in our response to valenced information.

Recognizing variation in the extent to which both news producers and news consumers are drawn to negativity helps explain the trends depicted in Figure 1 and 2. This variation also highlights the increasing viability of positively valenced news content – a consequence of the changing "space" for news and the changing access to positively (and negatively) valenced content in an increasingly high-choice media environment. Moreover, this increased viability of positive news points to actionable findings for individuals and organizations involved in news making and dissemination.

Consider the news environment as we complete this Element one week after the 2020 election. COVID-19 cases are rising in the United States and around the world. All reputable news agencies have declared Joe Biden the next president, although there is as yet no concession from President Trump. Trump has thus far refused to state his commitment to a peaceful transition of power and maintains that the election results are a hoax perpetrated by some combination of senior Democrats, the fake media, and corrupt bureaucrats. There is plenty of negatively valenced news, to be sure.

At the same time, we have also seen a lot of coverage of Major and Champ, the Bidens' two dogs. We've learned that Champ was Biden's dog when Biden was the vice president, and we've learned that Major will be the first shelter dog to live in the White House (Wertheim 2020). Perhaps it is the absence of other details about the transition, or the need for something novel, or the need for adaptive processing. Regardless, Major and Champ have for the past several days featured regularly in traditional and social media alike. (They are, we admit, highly Instagram-able – within days of the 2020 election being officially called, the dogs already had unofficial Twitter and Instagram accounts.)

One lesson of recent news coverage is that even when there is plenty of negatively valenced content, and even when news producers are not necessarily committed to prioritizing positively valenced content, positive news still finds a way. Positive content is not a rare and unattended anomaly, but rather a regular and predictable outcome of the way in which humans process information. When faced with limited space and time, news organizations have to focus on the most critical information, and that information will in many instances be negatively valenced. But changes in technology increasingly mean that space and time for news are less limited. Attracting an audience in a high-choice news environment and keeping that audience interested and informed can (and sometimes does) proceed with these facts in mind.

It is unlikely that knowing about Major and Champ is important in order to hold the Biden administration accountable for its campaign promises. That said, Major and Champ may increase the possibility that people may pay a bit more attention to the news and learn enough to know about campaign promises. And it need not always be the case that news content is either important *or* positive. A happy story for the sake of adaptive processing is worthwhile; so too is a positively valenced story about a fulfilled policy objective or improving economy, or a story that incorporates a combination of negative and positive features – as is the case for many stories about the ways in which individuals are successfully coping with socially distancing during the pandemic, for instance. The seriousness of news content need not be damaged by a commitment to more readily available positive content.

Note that there are parallels between this argument and those made in the literature on political humor. (For a useful review, see Young 2017.) The literature on "soft news" such as infotainment programming and late-night talk shows has debated whether this kind of programming serves as a kind of gateway to political knowledge for people who might otherwise not attend to politics (e.g., Baum 2003; Prior 2003; Xenos and Becker 2009). The distinction between soft and hard news is about much more than valence, of course, but it is nevertheless true that hard news tends to be negatively valenced while soft news tends to be positively valenced. Recent work on late-night programs highlights the ways in which late-night comedy tries to process largely negative news in a more positive light (e.g., Farnsworth and Lichter 2019). Other research emphasizes the positive impact of satire or parody programs, rather than late-night talk shows, as a source of political interest and efficacy (Hoffman and Young 2011). All of this work buttresses, in our view, the argument that positively valenced content may help rather than preclude attentiveness to "serious" political issues.

Moreover, the ready supply of information that is both negatively and positively valenced, and easily accessed by audience members with variable valence-based preferences, seems to us an especially effective means by which news media can fulfill their Fourth Estate obligation. One past argument in support of negative content is that it may sustain attentiveness to political issues (e.g., Soroka 2014). The same could be said of positive content, depending on the context. The challenge for news makers moving forward is to reconsider news making and newsworthiness in a way that is less focused on the average audience member and more adaptable to variation across audience members. Our suspicion is that doing so may lead to an increased audience for political news content.

That said, the proliferation of positively valenced news coverage does not depend on media organizations alone. News organizations (and social media companies) can certainly contribute to a shift in the valence of news content, but they are also increasingly forced to contend with diverse audience preferences. Human variation (both time-varying and stable) in valence-based biases has been and may increasingly be evident in our attentiveness to and recirculation of news content. Put another way, people share the stories that they believe are important and that they believe others should want to read. Whether that story is about the new COVID-19 taskforce formed as part of the presidential transition or about Major and Champ however, depends both on the person doing the sharing and the informational context. When much of the news is negative, the possibility that presidential dogs (or skiing squirrels) offer people some means of dealing with that negativity may allow platforms to retain audiences that may otherwise start to avoid news altogether. And when there is seemingly infinite space for information, stories about dogs and squirrels do not mean less space for stories with important implications for people's welfare.

Regardless of their news interests and platform preferences, people need positive content. (Although how much positive content they need varies.) It is this human need for positive content that produces happier stories at the end of evening broadcasts, the relatively quick recovery in news coverage after negative events, and the long-term limit to negativity in media content. Human nature has been the mechanism behind the self-correcting valence of news coverage. Given recent technological change, human nature may well produce an increase in the availability of positive news as well.

Bibliography

Altheide, David L. 1997. "The News Media, the Problem Frame, and the Production of Fear." *Sociological Quarterly* 38: 647–68.

Aslama, Minna, Heikki Hellman, and Tuomo Sauri. 2004. "Does Market-Entry Regulation Matter? Competition in Television Broadcasting and Programme Diversity in Finland, 1993–2002." *Gazette* (Leiden, Netherlands) 66(2): 113–32.

Bachleda, Sarah, Fabian Neuner, Stuart Soroka et al. 2020. "Individual-Level Differences in Negativity Biases in News Selection." *Personality and Individual Differences* 155: 109675.

Bakker, Bert N., Gijs Schumacher, Claire Gothreau, and Kevin Arceneaux. 2020. "Conservatives and Liberals Have Similar Physiological Responses to Threats." *Nature Human Behaviour* 4(6): 613–21.

Baum, Matthew A. 2003. "Soft News and Political Knowledge: Evidence of Absence or Absence of Evidence?" *Political Communication* 20, 173–90.

Bayer, Mareike, Werner Sommer, and Annekathrin Schacht. 2010. "Reading Emotional Words within Sentences: The Impact of Arousal and Valence on Event-Related Potentials." *International Journal of Psychophysiology* 78 (3): 299–307.

Benoit, Kenneth, Kohei Watanabe, Haiyan Wang, Paul Nulty, Adam Obeng, Stefan Muller, and Akitaka Matsuo. 2018. "quanteda: An R Package for the Quantitative Analysis of Textual Data." *Journal of Open Source Software* 3(30): 774.

Benoit, William L., Kevin A. Stein, and Glenn J. Hansen. 2005. "*New York Times* Coverage of Presidential Campaigns." *Journalism & Mass Communication Quarterly* 82(2): 356–76.

Berger, Jonah, and Katherine Milkman. 2012. "What Makes Online Content Viral?" *Journal of Marketing Research* 49(2): 192–205.

Bodas, Moran, Maya Siman-Tov, Kobi Peleg, and Zahava Solomon. 2015. "Anxiety-Inducing Media: The Effect of Constant News Broadcasting on the Well-Being of Israeli Television Viewers." *Psychiatry* 78(3): 265–76.

Bossetta, Michael. 2018. "The Digital Architectures of Social Media: Comparing Political Campaigning on Facebook, Twitter, Instagram, and Snapchat in the 2016 U.S. Election." *Journalism & Mass Communication Quarterly* 95(2): 471–96.

Brader, Ted. 2006. *Campaigning for Hearts and Minds: How Emotional Appeals in Political Ads Work*. Chicago: University of Chicago Press.

Cappella, Joseph N., and Kathleen Hall-Jamieson. 1997. *Spiral of Cynicism: The Press and the Public Good.* New York: Oxford University Press.

Carroll, Glenn R. 1985. "Concentration and Specialization: Dynamics of Niche Width in Populations of Organizations." *American Journal of Sociology* 90(6): 1262–83.

Chadwick, Andrew. 2013. *The Hybrid Media System: Politics and Power.* Oxford: Oxford University Press.

Chambers, Todd. 2003. "Radio Programming Diversity in the Era of Consolidation." *Journal of Radio Studies* 10(1): 33–45.

Dalton, Russell J., Paul A. Beck, and Robert Huckfeldt. 1998. "Partisan Cues and the Media: Information Flows in the 1992 Presidential Election." *American Political Science Review* 92(1): 111–26.

Damasio, Antonio. 2005. *Descartes' Error: Emotion, Reason, and the Human Brain.* New York: Penguin Group US.

Davie, William R., and Jung-Sook Lee. 1995. "Sex, Violence, and Consonance/ Differentiation: An Analysis of Local TV News Values." *Journalism & Mass Communication Quarterly* 72(1): 128–38.

Diamond, Edwin. 1978. *Good News, Bad News.* Cambridge, MA: MIT Press.

Dragoi, Valentin, Jitendra Sharma, Earl K. Miller, and Mriganka Sur. 2002. "Dynamics of Neuronal Sensitivity in Visual Cortex and Local Feature Discrimination." *Nature Neuroscience* 5(9): 883–91.

Druckman, James N., Samara Klar, Yanna Krupnikov, Matthew Levendusky, and John Barry Ryan. 2021. "Affective Polarization, Local Contexts, and Public Opinion in America." *Nature Human Behaviour* 5: 28–38.

Dunaway, Johanna. 2008. "Markets, Ownership, and the Quality of Campaign News Coverage." *Journal of Politics* 70(4): 1193–1202.

2013. "Media Ownership and Story Tone in Campaign News." *American Politics Research* 41(1): 24–53.

Epstein, Seymour. 1994. "Integration of the Cognitive and the Psychodynamic Unconscious." *American Psychologist* 49(8): 709–24.

Fallows, James. 1997. *Breaking the News: How the Media Undermine American Democracy.* New York: Vintage.

Farnsworth, Stephen J., and S. Robert Lichter. 2019. *Late Night with Trump: Political Humor and the American Presidency.* New York: Routledge.

2007. *The Nightly News Nightmare: Television's Coverage of U.S. Presidential Elections, 1988–2004.* Lanham, MD: Rowman & Littlefield.

Fazio, Russell H., J. Richard Eiser, and Natalie J. Shook. 2004. "Attitude Formation through Exploration: Valence Asymmetries." *Journal of Personality and Social Psychology* 87(3): 293–311.

Feng, Chunliang et al. 2014. "Arousal Modulates Valence Effects on Both Early and Late Stages of Affective Picture Processing in a Passive Viewing Task." *Social Neuroscience* 9(4): 364–77.

Fiske, Susan T. 1980. "Attention and Weight in Person Perception: The Impact of Negative and Extreme Behavior." *Journal of Personality and Social Psychology* 38(6): 889–906.

Fournier, Patrick, Stuart Soroka, and Lilach Nir. 2020. "Negativity Biases and Political Ideology: A Comparative Test across 17 Countries." *American Political Science Review* 114(3): 775–91.

Fridkin, Kim L., and Patrick Kenney. 2011. "Variability in Citizens' Reactions to Different Types of Negative Campaigns." *American Journal of Political Science* 55(2): 307–25.

Gaspar, Rui, Cláudia Pedro, Panos Panagiotopoulos, and Beate Seibt. 2016. "Beyond Positive or Negative: Qualitative Sentiment Analysis of Social Media Reactions to Unexpected Stressful Events." *Computers in Human Behavior* 56: 179–91.

Geer, John G. 2008. *In Defense of Negativity: Attack Ads in Presidential Campaigns.* Chicago: University of Chicago Press. http://books.google.ca /books?id=pSMBRZ0ig-AC

Gianotti, Lorena R. et al. 2008. "First Valence, Then Arousal: The Temporal Dynamics of Brain Electric Activity Evoked by Emotional Stimuli." *Brain Topography* 20(3): 143–56.

Glasser, Theodore L. 1984. "Competition and Diversity among Radio Formats: Legal and Structural Issues." *Journal of Broadcasting* 28(2): 127–42.

Gooding, Richard Z., Sanjay Goel, and Robert M. Wiseman. 1996. "Fixed versus Variable Reference Points in the Risk-Return Relationship." *Journal of Economic Behavior & Organization* 29(2): 331–50.

Gortner, Eva-Maria, and James W. Pennebaker. 2003. "The Archival Anatomy of a Disaster: Media Coverage and Community-Wide Health Effects of the Texas A&M Bonfire Tragedy." *Journal of Social and Clinical Psychology* 22(5): 580–603.

Grant, August E. 1994. "The Promise Fulfilled? An Empirical Analysis of Program Diversity on Television." *Journal of Media Economics* 7(1): 51–64.

Guess, Andrew, Jonathan Nagler, and Joshua Tucker. 2019. "Less than You Think: Prevalence and Predictors of Fake News Dissemination on Facebook." *Science Advances* 5(1): eaau4586.

Harmon, Mark D. 1989. "Market Size and Local Television News Judgment." *Journal of Media Economics* 2(1): 15–29.

Hellman, Heikki. 2001. "Diversity: An End in Itself? Developing a Multi-measure Methodology of Television Programme Variety Studies." *European Journal of Communication* 16(2): 181–208.

Helson, Harry. 1964. *Adaptation-Level Theory: An Experimental and Systematic Approach to Behavior*. New York:Harper and Row.

Hey, John D. 1994. "Expectations Formation: Rational or Adaptive or . . . ?" *Journal of Economic Behavior & Organization* 25(3): 329–49.

Hiaeshutter-Rice, Daniel. 2020. *Political Platforms: Technology, User Affordances, and Campaign Communications*. Ann Arbor, MI: ProQuest Dissertations & Theses.

Hiaeshutter-Rice, Daniel and Brian Weeks. N.d. "Understanding Audience Engagement with Mainstream and Alternative News Posts on Facebook." Forthcoming in *Digital Journalism*.

Hibbing, John R., Kevin B. Smith, and John R. Alford. 2014. "Differences in Negativity Bias Underlie Variations in Political Ideology." *Behavioral and Brain Sciences* 37(3): 297–307.

Himelboim, Itai et al. 2016. "Valence-Based Homophily on Twitter: Network Analysis of Emotions and Political Talk in the 2012 Presidential Election." *New Media & Society* 18(7): 1382–1400.

Hofer, Matthias, and Allison Eden. 2020. "Successful Aging through Television: Selective and Compensatory Television Use and Well-Being." *Journal of Broadcasting & Electronic Media* 64(2): 131–49.

Hoffman, Lindsay H., and Dannagal G. Young. 2011. "Satire, Punch Lines, and the Nightly News: Untangling Media Effects on Political Participation." *Communication Research Reports* 28(2): 159–68.

Hofstetter, C. Richard, and David M. Dozier. 1986. "Useful News, Sensational News: Quality, Sensationalism and Local TV News." *Journalism & Mass Communication Quarterly* 63(4): 815–53.

Hopmann, David Nicolas, Rens Vliegenthart, Claes de Vreese, and Erik Albaek. 2010. "Effects of Election News Coverage: How Visibility and Tone Influence Party Choice." *Political Communication* 27(4): 389–405.

Humprecht, Edda, and Frank Esser. 2018. "Diversity in Online News." *Journalism Studies* 19(12): 1825–47.

Ito, Tiffany, and John Cacioppo. 2005. "Variations on a Human Universal: Individual Differences in Positivity Offset and Negativity Bias." *Cognition & Emotion* 19(1): 1–26.

Itti, Laurent, and Pierre Baldi. 2009. "Bayesian Surprise Attracts Human Attention." *Vision Research* 49(10): 1295–1306.

Iyengar, Shanto, Yphtach Lelkes, Matthew Levendusky, Neil Malhotra and Sean J. Westwood. 2019. "The Origins and Consequences of Affective

Polarization in the United States." *Annual Review of Political Science*. 22: 129–46.

Johnston, Wendy M., and Graham C. L. Davey. 1997. "The Psychological Impact of Negative TV News Bulletins: The Catastrophizing of Personal Worries." *British Journal of Psychology* 88(1): 85–91.

de Jong, Allard Sicco, and Benjamin J. Bates. 1991. "Channel Diversity in Cable Television." *Journal of Broadcasting & Electronic Media* 35(2): 159–66.

Jungherr, Andreas. 2015. *Analyzing Political Communication with Digital Trace Data: The Role of Twitter Messages in Social Science Research.* New York: Springer.

Just, Marion R., Ann N. Crigler, and W. Russell Neuman. 1996. "Cognitive and Affective Dimensions of Political Conceptualization." In *The Psychology of Political Communication*, ed. Ann N. Crigler. Ann Arbor: University of Michigan Press, 133–48.

Kahneman, Daniel. 2013. *Thinking, Fast and Slow*. 1st edition. New York: Farrar, Straus and Giroux.

Katz, Elihu, Jay G. Blumler, and Michael Gurevitch. 1973. "Uses and Gratifications Research." *Public Opinion Quarterly* 37(4): 509–23.

Kerbel, Matthew. 1995. *Remote and Controlled: Media Politics in a Cynical Age*. Boulder, CO: Westview Press.

Kim, Hyun Suk. 2015. "Attracting Views and Going Viral: How Message Features and News-Sharing Channels Affect Health News Diffusion." *Journal of Communication* 65(3): 512–34.

Kinnick, Katherine N., Dean M. Krugman, and Glen T. Cameron. 2016. "Compassion Fatigue: Communication and Burnout toward Social Problems." *Journalism & Mass Communication Quarterly* 73(3): 687–707.

Kraft, Patrick, Yanna Krupnikov, Kerri Milita, John Ryan, and Stuart Soroka. 2020. "Social Media and the Changing Information Environment: Sentiment Differences in Read versus Re-Circulated News Content." *Public Opinion Quarterly* 84(S1): 195–215.

Krupnikov, Yanna. 2014. "How Negativity Can Increase and Decrease Voter Turnout: The Effect of Timing." *Political Communication* 31(3): 446–66.

2011. "When Does Negativity Demobilize? Tracing the Conditional Effect of Negative Campaigning on Voter Turnout." *American Journal of Political Science* 55(4): 797–813.

Krupnikov, Yanna, and Spencer Piston. 2015. "Accentuating the Negative: Candidate Race and Campaign Strategy." *Political Communication* 32 (1): 152–73.

Lamberson, PJ and Stuart Soroka. 2018. "A Model of Attentiveness to Outlying News." *Journal of Communication* 68(5): 942–64.

Lengauer, Günther, Frank Esser, and Rosa Berganza. 2012. "Negativity in Political News: A Review of Concepts, Operationalizations and Key Findings." *Journalism* 13(2): 179–202.

Lichter, S. Robert, and Richard E. Noyes. 1996. *Good Intentions Make Bad News: Why Americans Hate Campaign Journalism.* Lanham, MD: Rowman & Littlefield.

Loewenstein, George F., Elke U. Weber, Christopher K. Hsee, and Ned Welch. 2001. "Risk As Feelings." *Psychological Bulletin* 127(2): 267–86.

Lowe, Will, Kenneth Benoit, Slava Mikhaylov, and Michael Laver. 2011. "Scaling Policy Preferences from Coded Political Texts." *Legislative Studies Quarterly* 36(1): 123–55.

Marin, Marie-France et al. 2012. "There Is No News Like Bad News: Women Are More Remembering and Stress Reactive after Reading Real Negative News than Men." *PLoS ONE* 7(10): e47189.

Moskalenko, Sophia, and Steven J. Heine. 2003. "Watching Your Troubles Away: Television Viewing As a Stimulus for Subjective Self-Awareness." *Personality and Social Psychology Bulletin* 29(1): 76–85.

Moy, Patricia, and Michael Pfau. 2000. *With Malice toward All? The Media and Public Confidence in Democratic Institutions.* Westport, CT: Praeger.

Nabi, Robin L. 1999. "A Cognitive-Functional Model for the Effects of Discrete Negative Emotions on Information Processing, Attitude Change, and Recall." *Communication Theory* 9: 292–320.

Napoli, Philip M. 1999. "Deconstructing the Diversity Principle." *Journal of Communication* 49(4): 7–34.

1997. "Rethinking Program Diversity Assessment: An Audience-Centered Approach." *Journal of Media Economics* 10(4): 59–74.

Newton, Kenneth. 1999. "Mass Media Effects: Mobilization or Media Malaise?" *British Journal of Political Science* 29(4): 577–99.

Niven, David. 2000. "The Other Side of Optimism: High Expectations and the Rejection of Status Quo Politics." *Political Behavior* 22(1): 71–88.

Norris, Catherine J., Jeff T. Larsen, L. Elizabeth Crawford, and John T. Cacioppo. 2011. "Better (or Worse) for Some than Others: Individual Differences in the Positivity Offset and Negativity Bias." *Journal of Research in Personality* 45(1): 100–11.

Parmelee, John H., and Nataliya Roman. 2019. "Insta-politicos: Motivations for Following Political Leaders on Instagram." *Social Media + Society.* 5(2). https://doi.org/10.1177/2056305119837662

Patterson, Thomas E. 1994. *Out of Order*. New York: Vintage Books.

Petersen, Michael Bang, Mathias Osmundsen, and Kevin Arceneaux. 2020. "The 'Need for Chaos' and Motivations to Share Hostile Political Rumors." https://psyarxiv.com/6m4ts/ (May 29, 2020).

Powers, Matthew, and Rodney Benson. 2014. "Is the Internet Homogenizing or Diversifying the News? External Pluralism in the U.S., Danish, and French Press." *International Journal of Press/Politics* 19(2): 246–65.

Prior, Markus. 2003. "Any Good News in Soft News? The Impact of Soft News Preference on Political Knowledge." *Political Communication* 20(2): 149–71.

2005. "News vs. Entertainment: How Increasing Media Choice Widens Gaps in Political Knowledge and Turnout." *American Journal of Political Science*. 49(3): 577–92.

2007. *Post-Broadcast Democracy: How Media Choice Increases Inequality in Political Involvement and Polarizes Elections*. New York: Cambridge University Press.

Proksch, Sven-Oliver, Will Lowe, Jens Wäckerle, and Stuart Soroka. 2019. "Multilingual Sentiment Analysis: A New Approach to Measuring Conflict in Legislative Speeches." *Legislative Studies Quarterly* 44(1): 97–131.

Robinson, Michael. 1976. "American Political Legitimacy in an Era of Electronic Journalism: Reflections on the Evening News." In *Television As a Social Force*, ed. Douglas Cater and Richard Adler. New York: Praeger, 97–139.

Roessler, Patrick. 2007. "Media Content Diversity: Conceptual Issues and Future Directions for Communication Research." *Annals of the International Communication Association* 31(1): 464–520.

Rosenbusch, Hannes, Anthony M. Evans, and Marcel Zeelenberg. 2019. "Multilevel Emotion Transfer on YouTube: Disentangling the Effects of Emotional Contagion and Homophily on Video Audiences." *Social Psychological and Personality Science* 10(8): 1028–35.

Ryu, Jung S. 1982. "Public Affairs and Sensationalism in Local TV News Programs." *Journalism & Mass Communication Quarterly* 59(1): 74–137.

Sabato, Larry. 1991. *Feeding Frenzy: How Attack Journalism Has Transformed American Politics*. New York: Free Press.

Shaw, Daron R. 1999. "The Impact of News Media Favorability and Candidate Events in Presidential Campaigns." *Political Communication* 16(2): 183–202.

Sheldon, Pavica, and Katherine Bryant. 2016. "Instagram: Motives for Its Use and Relationship to Narcissism and Contextual Age." *Computers in Human Behavior* 58: 89–97.

Sherif, Muzafer, and Carolyn W. Sherif. 1967. "Attitudes As the Individual's Own Categories: The Social Judgement Approach to Attitude Change." In *Attitude, Ego Involvement, and Change*, ed. Carolyn W. Sherif and Muzafer Sherif. New York: Wiley, 105–39.

Shook, Natalie J., and Russell H. Fazio. 2009. "Political Ideology, Exploration of Novel Stimuli, and Attitude Formation." *Journal of Experimental Social Psychology* 45(4): 995–98.

Skinner, Ellen A., Kathleen Edge, Jeffrey Altman, and Hayley Sherwood. 2003. "Searching for the Structure of Coping: A Review and Critique of Category Systems for Classifying Ways of Coping." *Psychological Bulletin* 129(2): 216–69.

Skowronski, John J., and Donal E. Carlston. 1989. "Negativity and Extremity Biases in Impression Formation: A Review of Explanations." *Psychological Bulletin* 105(1): 131–42.

Slovic, Paul, Melissa Finucane, Ellen Peters, and Donald G. MacGregor. 2002. "Rational Actors or Rational Fools: Implications of the Affect Heuristic for Behavioral Economics." *Journal of Socio-economics* 31(4): 329–42.

Song, Yunya, Xin-Yu Dai, and Jia Wang. 2016. "Not All Emotions Are Created Equal: Expressive Behavior of the Networked Public on China's Social Media Site." *Computers in Human Behavior* 60: 525–33.

Soroka, Stuart N. 2012. "The Gatekeeping Function: Distributions of Information in Media and the Real World." *Journal of Politics* 74(2): 514–28.

2006. "Good News and Bad News: Asymmetric Responses to Economic Information." *Journal of Politics* 68(2): 372–85.

2014. *Negativity in Democratic Politics: Causes and Consequences*. New York: Cambridge University Press.

Soroka, Stuart, Mark Daku, Dan Hiaeshutter-Rice, Lauren Guggenheim, and Josh Pasek. 2017. "Negativity and Positivity Biases in Economic News Coverage: Traditional versus Social Media." *Communication Research* 45(7): 1078–98.

Soroka, Stuart, Lauren Guggenheim and Dominic Valentino. N.d. "Valence-Based Biases in News Selection," currently online in 'Advance Articles' in the *Journal of Media Psychology*.

Soroka, Stuart, Marc André Bodet, Lori Young, and Blake Andrew. 2009. "Campaign News and Vote Intentions." *Journal of Elections, Public Opinion and Parties* 19(4): 359–76.

Soroka, Stuart, Patrick Fournier, and Lilach Nir. 2019. "Cross-National Evidence of a Negativity Bias in Psychophysiological Reactions to News." *Proceedings of the National Academy of Sciences* 116(38): 18888–92.

Soroka, Stuart N., Dominik A. Stecula, and Christopher Wlezien. 2015. "It's (Change in) the (Future) Economy, Stupid: Economic Indicators, the Media, and Public Opinion." *American Journal of Political Science* 59 (2): 457–74.

Steinberg, Brian. 2018. "Lester Holt Wants to Tell New Stories for 'NBC Nightly News' Sign-Off." *Variety.* https://variety.com/2018/tv/news/les ter-holt-sign-off-stories-nbc-nightly-news-1202835819/ (June 15, 2020).

Sterman, John D. 1987. "Systems Simulation. Expectation Formation in Behavioral Simulation Models." *Behavioral Science* 32(3): 190–211.

Strömbäck, Jesper, and Adam Shehata. 2010. "Media Malaise or a Virtuous Circle? Exploring the Causal Relationships between News Media Exposure, Political News Attention and Political Interest." *European Journal of Political Research* 49(5): 575–97.

Stroud, Natalie Jomini. 2011. *Niche News: The Politics of News Choice.* Oxford: Oxford University Press. www.oxfordscholarship.com/view/10 .1093/acprof:oso/9780199755509.001.0001/acprof-9780199755509 (January 12, 2019).

Szabo, Attila, and Katey L. Hopkinson. 2007. "Negative Psychological Effects of Watching the News in the Television: Relaxation or Another Intervention May Be Needed to Buffer Them!" *International Journal of Behavioral Medicine* 14(2): 57–62.

Taylor, Shelley E., and Annette L. Stanton. 2007. "Coping Resources, Coping Processes, and Mental Health." *Annual Review of Clinical Psychology* 3 (1): 377–401.

Thelwall, Mike. 2010. "Emotion Homophily in Social Network Site Messages." *First Monday.* https://journals.uic.edu/ojs/index.php/fm/article/view/2897 (July 20, 2020).

Tiffany, Kaitlyn. "The Women Making Conspiracy Theories Beautiful." *The Atlantic.* www.theatlantic.com/technology/archive/2020/08/how-insta gram-aesthetics-repackage-qanon/615364/ (November 6, 2020).

Trussler, Marc, and Stuart Soroka. 2014. "Consumer Demand for Cynical and Negative News Frames." *International Journal of Press/Politics* 19(3): 360–79.

Turetsky, Kate M. and Travis A. Riddle. 2018. "Porous Chambers, Echoes of Valence and Stereotypes: A Network Analysis of Online News Coverage Interconnectedness Following a Nationally Polarizing Race-Related Event." *Social Psychological and Personality Science* 9(2): 163–75.

Van Atteveldt, Wouter, Mariken A. C. G. van der Velden, and Mark Boukes. N.d. "The Validity of Sentiment Analysis: Comparing Manual Annotation, Crowd-Coding, Dictionary Approaches, and Machine

Learning Algorithms." Currently online in *Communication Methods and Measures*.

VanderWeele, Tyler J., and Arthur C. Brooks. 2020. "A Public Health Approach to Negative News Media: The 3-to-1 Solution." *American Journal of Health Promotion*. 0890117120914227.

Valentino, Nicholas A., Matthew N. Beckmann, and Thomas A. Buhr. 2001. "A Spiral of Cynicism for Some: The Contingent Effects of Campaign News Frames on Participation and Confidence in Government." *Political Communication* 18(4): 347–67.

Valentino, Nicholas A., Krysha Gregorowicz, and Eric W. Groenendyk. 2009. "Efficacy, Emotions and the Habit of Participation." *Political Behavior* 31(3): 307–30.

Victor, Daniel. 2018. "How Instagram Rose into a Cultural Powerhouse (Published 2018)." *New York Times*. www.nytimes.com/2018/09/25/tech nology/instagram-celebrities-cultural-powerhouse.html (November 6, 2020).

Vizcarrondo, Tom. 2013. "Measuring Concentration of Media Ownership: 1976–2009." *International Journal on Media Management* 15(3): 177–95.

de Vreese, Claes H. 2005. "The Spiral of Cynicism Reconsidered." *European Journal of Communication* 20(3): 283–301.

Waterloo, Sophie F., Susanne E. Baumgartner, Jochen Peter, and Patti M. Valkenburg. 2018. "Norms of Online Expressions of Emotion: Comparing Facebook, Twitter, Instagram, and WhatsApp." *New Media & Society* 20(5): 1813–31.

Wettheim, Bonnie. November 10, 2020. "Dog People Are Loving This (at Least Some of Them)." *New York Times*.

Wlezien, Christopher, and Stuart Soroka. 2018. "Mass Media and Electoral Preferences during the 2016 US Presidential Race." *Political Behavior* 41: 945–70.

Wolfers, Lara N., and Frank M. Schneider. N.d. "Using Media for Coping: A Scoping Review." Forthcoming in *Communication Research*.

Wormwood, Jolie Baumann et al. 2019. "Psychological Impact of Mass Violence Depends on Affective Tone of Media Content." *PLoS ONE* 14 (4). https://doi.org/10.1371/journal.pone.0213891

Xenos, Michael A., and Becker, Amy B. 2009. "Moments of Zen: Effects of *The Daily Show* on Information Seeking and Political Learning." *Political Communication*, 26, 317–32.

Young, Dannagal G. 2017. "Theories and Effects of Political Humor." *The Oxford Handbook of Political Communication*. 10.1093/oxfordhb/ 9780199793471.013.29_update_001

Young, Lori, and Stuart N. Soroka. 2012. "Affective News: The Automated Coding of Sentiment in Political Texts." *Political Communication* 29: 205–31.

Zajonc, Robert B. 1980. "Feeling and Thinking: Preferences Need No Inferences." *American Psychologist* 35(2): 151–75.

Zillmann, Dolf. 1988. "Mood Management through Communication Choices." *American Behavioral Scientist* 31(3): 327–40.

Politics and Communication

Stuart Soroka
University of Michigan
Stuart Soroka is currently the Michael W. Traugott Collegiate Professor of Communication and Media & Political Science, and Research Professor in the Center for Political Studies at the Institute for Social Research, University of Michigan. As of July 2021, he will be Professor of Communication at the University of California, Los Angeles. His research focuses on political communication, the sources and/or structure of public preferences for policy, and the relationships between public policy, public opinion, and mass media. His books include *Negativity in Democratic Politics* (2014) and *Degrees of Democracy* (with Christopher Wlezien, 2010), both with Cambridge University Press.

About the Series
Cambridge Elements in Politics and Communication publishes research focused on the intersection of media, technology, and politics. The series emphasizes forward-looking reviews of the field, path-breaking theoretical and methodological innovations, and the timely application of social-scientific theory and methods to current developments in politics and communication around the world.

Cambridge Elements ☰

Politics and Communication

Elements in the Series

Printed in the United States
by Baker & Taylor Publisher Services